NURTURING NEURODIVERGENCE

The Late-Identified Adults' Guide to Building
Healthy Relationships with Self and Others

Jasmine K. Y. Loo

E8F34T3H5

Nurturing Neurodivergence: The Late-Identified Adults' Guide to Building Healthy Relationships with Self and Others / Jasmine K. Y. Loo
ISBN: 978-0-6458960-8-4

Medical and Legal Disclaimers

All the content in this book is for informational or educational purposes only, and does not constitute a psychological service or medical advice. Always seek the guidance of your doctor or other qualified health professionals with all matter pertaining to your mental and physical health.

Never disregard the advice of a medical or mental health professional, or delay in seeking it because of something you have read in this book. If you are experiencing a medical emergency, please call your doctor, go to the nearest hospital emergency department, or call emergency services immediately.

The content of the book may provide links to other company websites and resources as a reference for you. Jasmine Loo Psychology (JLP) and the author do not endorse any product, and are not responsible for the accuracy, quality or suitability of any linked websites.

JLP and the author accept no responsibility permitted by law for how any individual use the information presented in this book for the purpose of claims, compensation, litigation, damages or personal problems.

JLP and the author make no representations or warranties, express or implied, about the completeness, accuracy, reliability, suitability or availability with respect to the information, products, services, or related graphics contained in this book for any purpose. Any use of this information is at your own risk.

DEDICATION

To my much-adored ND husband, who has been by my side through mild, sunny days and days when we're hit by cyclones, and all the days in between. Thank you for meeting my long stretches of being in hyperfocus, especially over the course of writing this book, with kindness and understanding.

To my beloved mentor, who has never so much as blinked an eye at any of my differences, and instead told me (more than once), "I don't think that's such a crazy idea after all". I sometimes think that my lifetime of interpersonal-rocky-road was to save up all the luck I'd need in exchange for having known you as my mentor. Thank you, from the bottom of my heart.

To my six-year-old self, who decided she'll one day become a psychologist before she knew the word itself, and (thanks to our one-track-mindedness) never stopped working towards that, regardless of any naysayers and hurdles.

To all the most spectacular NDs I've worked with (if you're wondering if this includes you, yes, it definitely does) – you're the reason why I'm still excited to head to work, even on the toughest, most exhausting of days. I'm sure most of you can relate to how hard that actually is. And for that, I thank *you*.

To all those who have supported me through my journey as a person, a psychologist, and an author,

To all my fellow quirky, out-of-place, vibrantly colourful neuro-kin whom I've yet to meet,

I appreciate you, and this book is dedicated to all of you.

Nurturing Neurodivergence is an essential resource for late-identified neurodivergent individuals, health professionals, or really anyone working with neurodivergent adults. During my early career as a psychologist, although I had an interest in neurodivergent adults and was even working in settings where I assessed and supported many, very few written resources existed. The resources that did exist typically focused on children, ignoring the fact that neurodivergent children eventually become neurodivergent adults (or worse, suggesting that they would "grow out of it"). More so, the idea that there were neurodivergent health professionals who had valuable insights to offer from their lived experience, in addition to their professional training and knowledge, was almost non-existent. In this book, Jasmine explores the many facets of what it means to be neurodivergent, whilst offering realistic strategies and ideas to help neurodivergent adults work with the brain they have – not against it.

Emmalee Stefanatos, Psychologist & Board-Approved Supervisor, Founder of Infinity Psychology & Assessments, BA (Psych), GDipPsych, MEd&DevPsych

Navigating a conversation in a foreign language is tough. Navigating a strange city without a map is tough. Navigating a (largely) neurotypical world is also really tough, especially when you don't speak the language or have the map. If you are a late-identified neurodivergent adult, or even a family member or friend of a late-identified neurodivergent adult, then Nurturing Neurodivergence is the guidebook that you need. Drawing on a wealth of lived experience, clinical training and knowledge, and research literature, Jasmine Loo has created a practical resource to help guide you in understanding your neurodivergence; navigating the complexities of relationships with others; and most importantly, with yourself.

Dr Shane Costello, Adjunct Senior Lecturer at Monash University, Australia, Educational & Developmental Psychologist, Board-Approved Supervisor

CONTENTS

INTRODUCTION

Getting the Most Out of This Book

With better self-understanding, we are better equipped to take life challenges in our own stride, and to build upon our self-acceptance. Finding out that you're neurodivergent doesn't take away any of your problems in life, change your past, or give you any guaranties about your future. But what this knowledge can help with is to offer you a point of reference in understanding your past and navigating your present, so you can look at your life through neurodivergent lenses. *Lenses that fit.*

Imagine if you've been wearing glasses all your life to help you see your way but you're still really struggling. Everything feels blurry and out of focus, and you keep stumbling and tripping over. One day, you found out that the lenses on your glasses were for short-sightedness but you actually have all along is long-sightedness. Getting lenses that fit doesn't mean life will then work itself out for you – no, you're still the only who can take life on, one step at a time – but you can at least have better clarity while you're at it. It is a lot easier to avoid stumbling and tripping over hazards if you can see them! Therefore, this book is intended to help bring clarity to your experience with neurodivergence.

Section I looks into the diverse profiles in autism and ADHD, and if you identify with one of them but not the other, you're still strongly encouraged to go through both chapters because much of the information in one chapter will also be relevant for the other. In addition to being a guide, this also serves as a workbook that supports you to engage in meaningful reflections on different topics at your own pace.

Remember, this book is here to support you, it's not homework. Throughout this book, you'll find that the text for all the question prompts for your self-reflection will be in *italics and blue in colour, like this.* And the text for all the activity and reading instructions (barring instructions on infographics) will be in orange, like this.

1

INTRODUCTION

For diagrams where you can fill out your answers to the activities and use as you would a mind map, some examples (non-exhaustive) can be found around the borders of each of those diagrams, if you would like some ideas. Otherwise, simply ignore them! Certain infographics in this book are available for free download in full-sized, high-resolution image files. Visit https://www.jasmine-loo.com/category/all-products, or simply scan the QR Code on the Copyrights page at the very front of this book, and enter the code "E8F34T3H5" at checkout for a 100% discount (i.e., free).

Troubleshooting some possible challenging scenarios

If you're an avid writer and the spaces provided for you to write on aren't enough, or if you'd really prefer not to write in books, consider writing your reflections on a separate notebook, with reference to the page numbers where the reflection prompts are. Typing them out (or using speech-to-text) in a document works, too. When possible, try to write your reflections after you've finished reading a particular section, so that the information that's related to the reflection prompts is still fresh in your mind.

If you're really keen to work through this book but struggle with motivation because of executive functioning challenges, try and see if you could arrange for something akin to 'body doubling' as a strategy to overcome this. For instance, you can consider making arrangements with a fellow ND friend (or a book club) to meet with you every week to work through parts of the book together. Buddying up can be really helpful with motivation.

If you happen to be reading this book at a time that you're burnt out and have limited resources, bear in mind you don't have to follow the order of the chapters. You may prefer to skip Section I and slowly go through Section II, for example. It's always OK to return to the rest at another time. Some of you may also be interested in working on the book with your mental health practitioner, if you find there's much more to unpack from the reflections you made. You can bring the book to your therapy sessions to help jog your memory on stuff you'd like to dive into within a safe therapy space.

The Ever-Changing Landscape of Neuro-Affirming Language

Neurodivergent people have existed throughout human history, but it's only been less than a hundred years since it was identified and documented (which we will discuss in Chap. 3). Advocacy for neurodivergence has really been making headway in the last decade or so, and the appropriate language in the context of discussing neurodivergence has been a contentious topic. It's an ever-changing landscape and so it should be. Ongoing reflection from society is necessary to ensure that we're always trying to better understand, represent and support the neurodivergent community.

Nevertheless, it's important to remember that even when there's a general consensus on the appropriate terms and language to use in discussing neurodivergence at any given time, those terms aren't going to work or make sense for every last neurodivergent person. Regardless of neurotype, we're all unique individuals with unique preferences and beliefs, after all. This is something that I always try to be mindful and be respectful of.

Having said all that, I acknowledge that in writing a book, it's impossible for any author to cater to everyone's unique preferences for, and beliefs of the most appropriate terms and language used in discussions of neurodivergence. This means that the language that I'll be using in this book will not work for everyone, to varying degrees, despite the best of intentions. It's also likely that what's defined as appropriate language at the time of writing may be different to what's ideal in future years.

You will find that while I don't discuss or look at neurodivergence using a deficit lens, I don't talk about it as a 'superpower' either. Any particular neurotype, just like race or gender, isn't inherently 'good' or 'bad'. Rather, what's crucial is to be empowered with self-knowledge, so we can more readily take on life's challenges. Hence, this book takes on a pragmatic approach, discussing the realistic side of what it means to be neurodivergent in a neurotypical world, in what I hope to be a compassionate way. I'm a believer of 'do what works'; so, if you find elements of this book helpful, feel free to adapt them to a language suitable for you.

INTRODUCTION
Language Used in This Book

Contractions and terms used

To help with the ease of reading, neurodivergent people (i.e., ASD and/or ADHD) will be referred to as '*NDs*', and neurotypical people as '*NTs*' in most of this book. 'Neurodivergence' in general also refers to many other conditions, but for the sake of defining a focused scope of discussion, these are the only two neurodivergent conditions discussed in this book. The term '*late-identified*', instead of 'late-diagnosed', is used to include both NDs who pursued a formal diagnosis in adulthood, and those who self-identified in adulthood without being formally diagnosed by health professionals. This term is specifically chosen for inclusion, and to acknowledge that not every late-identified ND would wish to, or be able to pursue formal diagnoses for a variety of reasons.

At times, 'people with ADHD' will also be referred to as '*ADHD-ers*'. Currently, the standard diagnostic guidebook called 'DSM-5-TR' – more on this later – refers to autism as 'autism spectrum disorder (ASD)', but many autistic people indicated a preference for the term 'autism'. This book attempts to present evidence-based, scientific research findings and clinical experience in a neuro-affirming manner. Therefore, in order to honour both of these intended purposes, this book will be using the terms '*autism' and 'ASD*' interchangeably, depending on context, to refer to individuals across the autism spectrum (which includes those previously diagnosed with 'Asperger's' or 'high/low-functioning autism' under old DSM categorisations).

Identity-first language

At the time that this book is written, many NDs indicated a preference for identity-first language (e.g., 'autistic person', instead of 'person with autism'), which is what this book will be using. However, on some occasions where '*ADHD-ers*' may be deemed to sound awkward, '*people with ADHD*' or '*adults with ADHD*' would be used instead. Check out the infographic on the next page for a list of definitions of other ND-related terms used in this book.

Neurodivergent Lingo

NEUROTYPE
The way someone's brain is wired, often associated with their neuro-developmental diagnosis or the lack thereof.

NEUROTYPICAL (NT)*
Refers to people without any neuro-developmental conditions/ diagnoses. NTs currently form the majority.

SPECIAL INTERESTS
A subject matter/ activity that NDs are intensely invested in and come to know a lot about. Some are long-term, others are more short-lived.

MELTDOWN
Emotional and/or sensory buildup and overload leading to explosive presentations (e.g., crying, screaming, self-injurious behaviours, etc).

MASKING
A form of coping mechanism where NDs learn to behave in ways that suppress their ND traits and appear more like NTs, in order to fit in/ not draw unwanted attention. Can be a result from being repeatedly told off/ shamed for ND traits.

NEURODIVERSE
Refers to people with **all different neurotypes**, incl. neurotypicals, autistic people, ADHD-ers, etc.

NEURODIVERGENT (ND)*
People whose brains are wired differently from the neurotype forming the majority (i.e., NTs), e.g., people with neuro-developmental conditions.

HYPERFOCUS
A state of being laser-focused on an activity/ subject matter. May not realise how much time's passed and might forget to eat, drink or shift body positions the whole time.

SHUTDOWN
Similar to meltdown, but presenting as an implosion (e.g., becoming unable to speak/ respond at all/ feeling unable to move, or needing to hide, or can only give autopilot responses, etc.).

STIMMING
Short for "self-stimulatory behaviours". Usually repetitive motions or actions that many NDs find calming, comforting or helps express emotions.

Are there any other ND terms that are significant/meaningful for you?

Taking Care of Yourself Emotionally

This book is a workbook-guide, with activities and questions that you can use for guided, introspective reflections. There are spaces for you to jot down your reflections. At times, reflecting on, or processing challenging experiences may bring about complex or intense emotions.

If you ever feel unsafe, please call emergency/mental health/suicide helpline numbers relevant to your region. If you don't know these numbers off the top of your head, search them up online now and write them below:

Important Numbers for Support

1.   Emergency number:

2.   Suicide helpline
Organisation name:
Operating hours:
Number:

3.   Mental health helpline
Organisation name:
Operating hours:
Number:

4.   My General Practitioner (GP)
Clinic name:
Operating hours:
Number:

5.   My Mental Health Practitioner
(e.g., psychologist / counsellor / psychiatrist, etc)
Clinic name:
Operating hours:
Number:

6.   My Trusted Friend or Family Member
Name: Number:
Name: Number:

SECTION I

UNDERSTANDING AUTISM & ADHD BEYOND THE MEDICAL MODEL

1.

FACES OF AUTISM

Don't get me wrong – being a scientist-practitioner, I get how much work from a huge team of researchers goes into each revision of the Diagnostic and Statistical Manual (DSM). The DSM is one of the two globally used standardised diagnostic handbook for a range of clinical conditions, including neurodevelopmental disorders, such as ASD and ADHD. It also forms the core of the medical model in understanding autism.

Understanding Autism Beyond the DSM-5-TR

The purpose of this chapter is not to discredit or to challenge the authority and validity of the DSM. Any attempts to encapsulate the substance of something extremely complex like autism, and condense it into something clear and concise would make an arduous process. At the same time, it's necessary because otherwise, there won't be a guide for clinicians all around the world to make consistent and reliable diagnoses with. It'll never be perfect, and it's one of the best that our scientists have currently come up with.

Before we try to move beyond something (or talk about why we should), however, we'd obviously need to get to know the thing we're trying to move beyond. So, first of all, let's take a look at the diagnostic criteria laid out in the current version of the DSM, known as the DSM-5-TR, using the infographic on the next page.

Autism Spectrum Disorder (ASD)

DSM-5-TR diagnostic criteria

Reference: American Psychiatric Association. (2022). Neurodevelopmental disorders. In Diagnostic and statistical manual of mental disorders (5th ed., text rev.).

I*. Ongoing difficulties in social communication and interactions shown in various situations, across all 3 of these areas:
- Trouble with showing the expected back-and-forth quality in social interactions, e.g., in conversations, or sharing of emotions.
- Challenges in showing and in interpreting non-verbal communication (e.g., maintaining eye contact, interpreting gestures)
- Struggles in forming and maintaining relationships, e.g., difficulty adjusting behaviours to different social contexts or showing little interest in others.

2*. Repeated patterns of behaviour, interests, or activities, characterised by 2 or more of these presentations:
- Unusual or repetitive behaviour using objects, hand movements or speech (e.g., repeatedly finger flicking, or saying certain phrases out of context).
- Strong preference for sameness in routines, as well as in ways of thinking, and behaving (e.g., adhering to the same bedtime routine)
- Interests that are unusually intense in degree and narrow in focus, e.g., being overly focused on specific objects or topics.
- Significantly heightened or decreased sensitivities to sensory input (e.g., being indifferent to pain or being bothered by specific sounds or tastes) or showing keen interest in seeking out particular sensory qualities from the environment.

3. Traits should have been present since early development, even if they only become apparent with increased social demands, or if they were masked by strategies acquired across development.

4. Symptoms significantly hinder a person's engagement in one or more major life domains (e.g., social, vocational/educational, emotional).

5. These symptoms cannot be fully accounted for by an intellectual developmental disorder or global developmental delay alone. Even though ASD may coexist with an intellectual disability, but to diagnose both, the social communication abilities should be below what is expected for the overall level of development.

*Specify if Level I (needing support), 2 (needing substantial support) or 3 (needing very substantial support)

1. FACES OF AUTISM

The DSM-5-TR very thoughtfully included reminders that their examples under each criterion are "illustrative, not exhaustive", and that autistic symptoms can be masked through acquired learning. Unfortunately, the reality is such that many people, medical and allied health professionals included, treat these more widely known ASD presentations as the only possible ASD presentations.

Autistic people who do not fit the stereotype, either because they have high social motivation (or are extraverted), or are able to demonstrate eye contact (or give the impression that they can) and engage in conversations, or work in careers involving a lot of interpersonal interactions, are often immediately dismissed because they "can't possibly be autistic".

*By simply looking at the DSM-5-TR criteria, how much do you think your presentation and experience fit or not fit the descriptions?*_____

_____

_____

_____

_____

_____

_____

_____

No, We Are *Not* "All a Bit Autistic"

One of the many things that many autistic people dread hearing from others is, "We're all a bit autistic, aren't we". A statement, not a question. A statement usually accompanied by a light-hearted chuckle. Most people probably do not say that out of a malicious place. Even so, that's enough to send many of us into a freeze mode from frustration because where do we even begin? So, hopefully, this infographic in the form of an autism mind map on the next page can help demonstrate that,

"No, we aren't all a bit autistic."

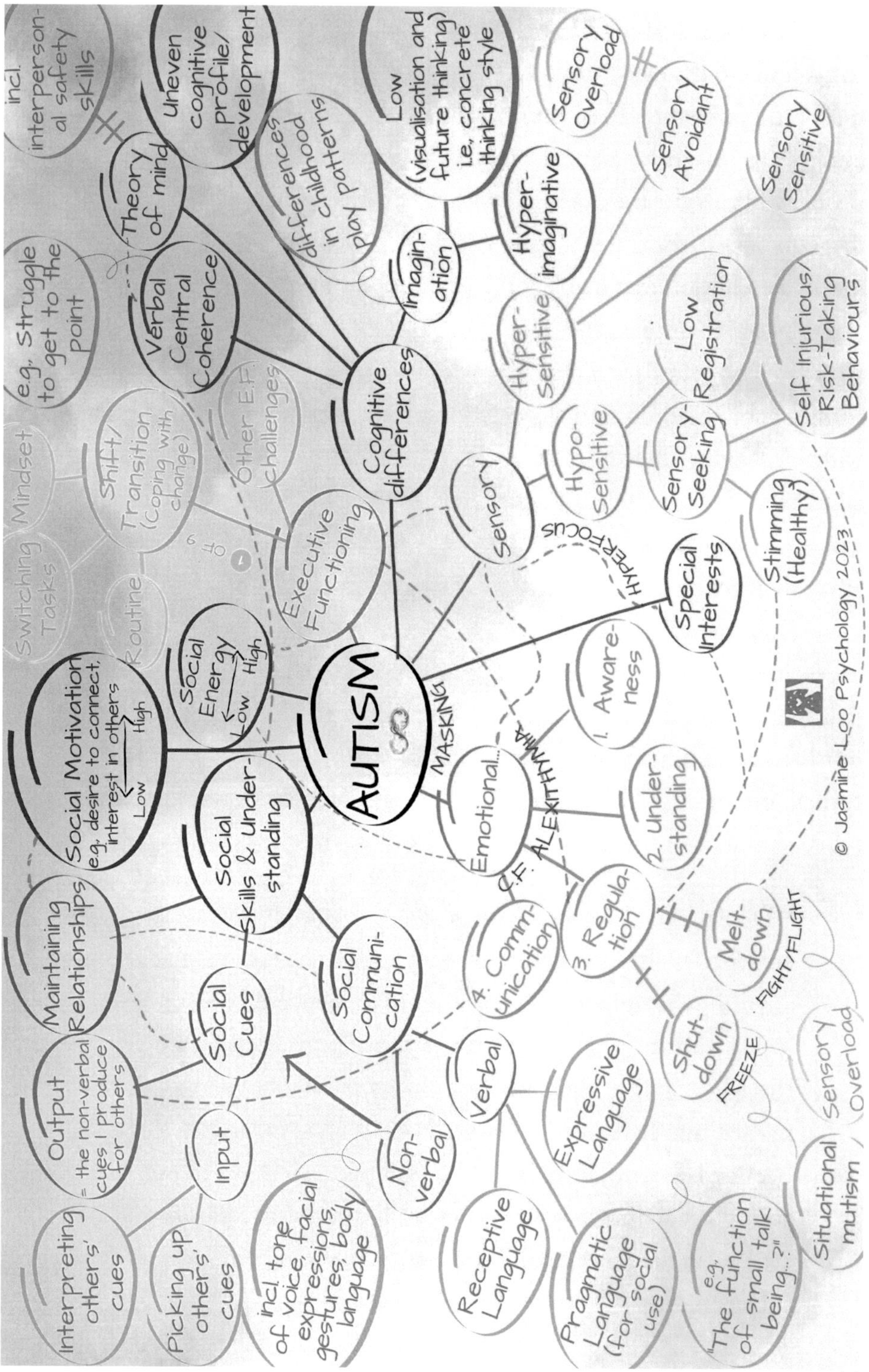
AUTISM
MASKING
Social Motivation e.g. desire to connect, interest in others
Low High
Social Energy
Low High
Social Skills & Understanding
Social Communication
Social Cues
Maintaining Relationships
Output = the non-verbal cues I produce for others
Input
Interpreting others' cues
Picking up others' cues
incl. tone of voice, facial expressions, gestures, body language
Non-verbal
Verbal
Receptive Language
Expressive Language
Pragmatic Language (for social use)
e.g. "The function of small talk being...?"
Situational mutism
Sensory Overload
Shut-down
FREEZE
Melt-down
FIGHT/FLIGHT
3. Regulation
4. Communication
Emotional...
C.F. ALEXITHYMIA
1. Awareness
2. Understanding
Special Interests
HYPERFOCUS
Stimming (Healthy)
Sensory
Sensory-Seeking
Self Injurious/ Risk-Taking Behaviours
Low Registration
Hypo-Sensitive
Hyper-Sensitive
Sensory Sensitive
Sensory Avoidant
Sensory Overload
Cognitive differences
Imagination
Hyper-imaginative
Low (visualisation and future thinking) i.e., concrete thinking style
differences in childhood play patterns
Uneven cognitive profile/ development
Theory of mind
incl. interpersonal safety skills
Verbal Central Coherence
e.g. Struggle to get to the point
Executive Functioning
Other E.F. challenges
Shift/ Transition (Coping with change)
Switching Tasks
Mindset
Routine
© Jasmine Loo Psychology 2023

1. FACES OF AUTISM

On the autism mind map, everyone probably experiences some of these struggles or traits every now and then, but an autistic person will experience most (and for some, all) of these traits and struggles to varying degrees. This is exactly the reason why autism is such a complex condition. No two autistic people will present the exact same way on this profile (i.e., basically the entire diagram above) because autism is a highly heterogenous condition, which means a condition that involves the mutation of more than one gene.

'More than one gene' would be an understatement. So far, hundreds of so called 'risk genes' for autism have been identified through large-scale genetic studies conducted on autistic individuals and their families. That, combined with this thing called "*epigenetics*", makes autism an incredibly complex condition for even scientific researchers to fully understand at this stage. Epigenetics is the study of how an individual's behaviours and environment affect their gene expression, or how their genes work.

Epigenetics show us that just because we carry a gene, it doesn't necessarily mean the gene will be expressed or manifested. We're all born with risk genes for different conditions, most of which won't even get activated in our lifetime. Think of gene expression as whether a particular gene ever gets turned 'on' or stays 'off', even when the gene itself is always there, unchanged (vs gene mutation, which is the abnormal changes in the genetic sequences).

> **Disclaimer: This is a very short and simple introduction to epigenetics. It's in _**NO**_ way implying or suggesting that there's anything that individuals, parents or families could do or not do to 'cause' autism. There's no single factor that causes autism - that's the whole point. Epigenetics is an incredibly fascinating subject matter, but there won't a full technical discussion on it in this book because this is not intended to be a genetics textbook. However, I'll strongly encourage that you search for peer-reviewed journal articles on the genetic studies and autism, if you're interested in the subject matter.

Autism has been found to involve both genetic mutations and epigenetic changes. THIS is the scientific reason behind the saying, "If you have met one autistic person, you have met one autistic person". It's not just a cliché. It is therefore important for all of us, especially health and mental health practitioners, to recognise the different faces of autism. Not fitting the stereotypical autism profile does not make a person any less autistic.

This is not to say that there's anything wrong with having a more widely known autism profile (e.g., Sheldon Cooper, Rain Man), but that it is harmful to the autistic community to *only* think of those profiles as 'fitting the bill'. It dismisses struggles and denies the very existence and identity of autistic people who do not present with profiles typically known.

On that note, if you ever feel tempted to say to an autistic person, "You don't look autistic" (most likely intended as a compliment), please think again. The diversity of it all is what adds colour and flavour to our world. I sincerely hope that we, as a society, will not just be 'aware' of neurodivergence, but also embrace and celebrate it.

Unpacking the Autism Mind Map

I won't be going into the widely known aspects of autism, but instead would like to introduce the non-stereotypical aspects of autism, which often relates to late-identified autistic individuals.

Social motivation and masking

The social motivation (blue area) levels of an autistic person tend to be one of the things that can make the biggest difference to their motivation in learning to 'mask' (c.f. infographic in the Introduction). It's sad that society still holds a stereotype of autistic people not wanting anything to do with anyone else, and would rather sit facing the corner of a room on their own.

Many autistic individuals deeply long for meaningful connections with others (even if they may struggle a lot with it), and this strong desire can be a

13

powerful driver behind the development of many masking behaviours that may be good enough to bring home an Oscar award. Studying what others do in social interactions, especially those who seem like they're good at it, then provides a framework for these autistic people to behave in ways that are 'more neurotypical' to help with fitting in.

Of course, this is by no means suggesting that the desire for connection and belongingness is the only or primary reason for ND masking. Many NDs mask because it's the only way they could have some hope at experiencing (actual and/or perceived) safety in a world where they're a minority because of their neurotype. You may notice on the mind map that 'masking' is simply placed beneath 'autism' because there isn't a spot to place it that makes complete sense – it permeates every area of neurodivergence. It's also why I didn't make up a separate chapter for the topic of masking. For this reason, adult diagnostic assessments are arguably more challenging to conduct than child diagnostic assessments because they require the assessing practitioner to have a deep and broad understanding of masking.

Some might think, "Everyone masks from time to time. I hide away the fact that I hated being at work every day, for instance. I pretend to find Uncle John funny at family gatherings. It's not all that unusual". Indeed, no one would present wholly as their true self 100% of the time, so what is different about neurodivergent masking? Perhaps a little snippet of what the thought process behind autistic masking can look like would be helpful.

"OK, Mary thought I was too direct the last time I shared my thoughts, so maybe I should let others give feedback instead and take mental notes. Oh no, John just cast me a look. Wait, was that directed at me? Maybe they did want me to say something. Argh, I can't tell from their faces. How many minutes has it been since I last spoke? Stop fidgeting, that definitely annoyed everyone. You know what? Just smile and nod. Get to work, facial muscles, you can do it. Can't go wrong with looking agreeable. Noooo, I probably nodded too rapidly and looked like a bobble head figurine."

This sort of thinking process is almost constant for many NDs who engage in daily masking. At this point, I'm almost certain there'd be some health professionals who'd think, "That's social anxiety, not autism!". Well, of course there's social anxiety involved (probably tonnes of it), but when social anxiety is almost exclusively tied to autistic struggles, such as difficulty reading social cues, past experiences of social mistakes/relational trauma and sensory processing difference, social anxiety is a secondary presentation. Autism is the primary.

Each and every one of us has as much of a choice in the neurotype we're born in as the colour of our skin. For many NDs, all we wanted is to belong somewhere, or just to feel safe in interpersonal situations. But sadly, often the reality is such that we pay the price of constant vigilance in monitoring every interpersonal move we make under a magnifying glass, in return for a 'maybe' in feeling a sense of belongingness.

So perhaps, just perhaps, a safe place of belongingness needs to reside within us, so that even in the roughest and loneliest of times, we can say, "I belong with me. I accept me. I can find a safe haven in me". It's undoubtably a long and arduous journey to build this, but hopefully at the end of this book, you'd think that you're one step closer.

Social understanding and theory of mind: It's not what you think

There have been many definitions of theory of mind (ToM; also 'mind-reading', 'social cognition' and 'social understanding') in the literature since its conception in the 70s', but my favourite based on clarity is this:

> *"The ability of an individual to make inferences about what others may be thinking or feeling and to predict what they may do in a given situation based on those inferences."*

Throughout the history of autism literature, ToM deficit has been considered to be one of the main explanations for the social struggles of autistic people, and there has been a lot of research studies showing the link between autism and ToM challenges.

One consistent theme that you might notice to be regularly showing up, though, is society's tendency to take the first (and most probably only) thing they know about a concept, along with research evidence related to the concept, and run with it. Chances are, they haven't examined the quality of the research studies. They may even only read the one sentence in each paper's conclusion, or may never have read the actual papers at all, and just ran with conclusions drawn up by others who have read the research, that may or may not be accurate.

Even though it's found that autistic people do indeed struggle with ToM (science speak: "statistically significant relationship"/ "p<.05"), a 2019 meta-analysis combining and analysing the findings from 133 research papers that examined the ToM-autism link found that the actual strength of this connection that gives us meaningful information (science speak: the "effect size") was, surprisingly, very small. ToM was found to help explain only 4.5% of the social functioning levels of autistic people. To put it simply, an autistic person's ToM ability only explains 4.5% of how they're doing socially. Fat load of help.

For many late-identified autistic adults, intelligence and high motivation to mask are major contributing factors that drive their social learning behaviours. Research showed that where instinctive ToM falls short, it may be compensated for by intelligence, executive functioning (e.g., motivation and sustained effort), and *a tonne of anxiety* (which supports the above section on masking).

In other words, the autistic person explicitly learns (i.e., using logical reasoning and executive functioning as compensation) how each scenario, or their own behaviours could affect other people, and stays on constant high alert to always be ready (i.e., anxiety as compensation) for engaging in this type of mental processing because ToM doesn't come naturally to them.

Autistic people often engage in explicit learning in social thinking as we would learn Physics at school. Obviously, even with their best efforts and intention, they will still not get it right every single time (after all, which allistic person would get it right all the time?), and others may think, "Gee, how inconsiderate". But if we preach "it's the thought that counts" in gift-giving culture, why do we never consider the pain and effort that may have gone into an autistic person's attempt to be considerate towards others? Food for thought. While we can't control how other people interpret our intentions and actions, we can at least give our chronically over-heating, working-way-too-hard brain a long overdue 'pat on the back'.

Nevertheless, even if the aforementioned is relatively well-managed for an autistic person who may step on others' toes minimally, the impact from ToM struggles on their social understanding may still come to bite them in the rear end. Clinical experience suggests that this may be a big reason why autistic people are at a much higher risk of being exploited or abused, compared to allistic people (further discussion in Chap. 4). Social safety skills rely heavily on social understanding and ToM.

An autistic person may be very bright and learn a lot of skills over the years to be more 'street-smart'. Or they may have already had a lot of past experience of being burnt from misjudging other people's agenda. However, since ToM doesn't come instinctively for them, their default mode may still be 'to see the world as they see it'. For example, if an autistic person's life view is that they would never take advantage of others and be deceitful, this would often be the default programming that they use in understanding others' agenda. They are likely to think, "If I'll never do that to a friend, someone I consider a friend will also never do that to me".

Of course, it'd hardly ever be a conscious reasoning process and a thought that is spelled out like in my example above. That's what instinctive ability is about, isn't it? The neurons in our brain fire at each other following a well-used neural pathway so quickly that we may not even be conscious of it. In certain situations where caution in naturally called for, such as making work decisions, or when entering a legal agreement, an autistic person may be more able to consciously steer away from their default mode and use the social knowledge they've acquired over the years to help them analyse the situation and hopefully make a right decision.

However, even if an autistic person has chronic, intense anxiety to compensate for ToM struggles, the human brain is not designed to literally stay in the highest alert *all the time*. There'll always be times and situations when we unconsciously lower our guard, for example in personal relationships. These are generally the times when we may not even be aware that we've automatically turned to our default programming and potentially misjudged a social situation. If we're unlucky, the lapse in judgement may also come with a hefty price tag to ourselves.

So, if you ever called yourself 'dumb' or 'stupid' for falling for the same interpersonal BS not once, but twice, and possibly even more times, know that it has nothing to do with your intelligence. I'm not saying let it all go and open yourself up to any exploitation, but that if you unfortunately relate to any of this, then please try to go easy on yourself. We do not have control over how rough life gets, or if the world offers us any compassion, but what we do have control over is whether we extend ourselves any compassion.

Another harmful myth that the autism-ToM link relates to is society's blanket assumption that ToM deficit must mean empathy deficit. If you struggle to instinctively infer others' thoughts and feelings, then surely, you're incapable of empathy, right? Wrong.

Just because a person may not instinctively know what another person is thinking about doesn't mean they don't care. Modern research has consistently been showing that social understanding (the thinking part) and empathy (the affective/emotional part) are two related but separate neurological processes. In fact, recent research demonstrated a higher tendency for autistic people to be hyper-empathic, despite ToM struggles. Chap. 7 will be discussing the interesting research findings pertaining to this in more detail.

This is not to say that all autistic people are empathetic either because we aren't all clone copies of each other. There are autistic people who are more empathetic, there are autistic people who are less empathetic. Exactly like how there are allistic (i.e., non-autistic) people who are more empathetic, and allistic people who are less empathetic.

Verbal central coherence

Central coherence is a fancy scientific name that describes the human capacity for 'big picture' processing (as contrasted with 'localised' processing that focuses on specific details). Traditionally, the research around the links between autism and central coherence has been focused much more on visual, or non-verbal central coherence.

Overall, the research outcome has been mixed, which suggests that this isn't an area that all autistic people struggle with. Remember how we were talking about autism being a highly heterogenous condition at the start of this chapter? Some autistic people may have adequate central coherence abilities.

What's less emphasised, and is only starting to emerge in autism research is 'verbal' central processing, or some researchers have called "event narrative" capacities. The reason why we are discussing it here is because clinical experience suggests that this is an area that some (definitely not all) autistic people struggle intensely with, and can significantly impact on the effectiveness of a person's social communication in their day-to-day. This means that for those impacted, it can have some serious real-life implications.

For instance, it's not uncommon for bright and articulate autistic children (up to around upper primary school age) to struggle with what may seem ordinary questions, such as, *"So, what do you do after school?"* In some severe cases, the child might respond with something like, *"I'll open the car door, get in the car, and we drive home. Then I open the car door, grab my bag, shut the door, and wait for mum to unlock our front door. I take off my shoes and socks, put away my bag, open the fridge door for a glass of cold water...".*

If the question was asked by an adult, this type of response may be misunderstood as the child trying to be 'smart', or 'trying to be funny'. The child might even be punished for it. If a peer had asked that question, sadly, there's a good chance that they might move away and do something else before the autistic child finished answering. It would appear that these result from a 'mash-up' between struggles in at least 3 areas on the mind map:

1. Verbal central coherence – flexibly 'zooming out' to look at the whole picture of the event, instead of individual components involved within the event to provide a summarised response appropriate to context,

2. Social understanding – knowing instinctively which specific part of what I do after school does the person asking the question really want to know about, or is interested in, and

3. Pragmatic language – effective use of language to successfully navigate a social interaction.

In autistic adults, severe struggles in this area might create a lot of social communication anxiety and frustrations. It may mean some degree of social withdrawal for some, but even then, situations calling for event narrative are almost inevitable. When we're required to give a police statement on an incident we witnessed, for example. When we'd like to share something stressful at work today with a friend, or communicate to our boss about the reason why we need to work from home after perhaps a family member had an accident and requires our care. If you frequently feel like you're simply unable to 'tell a story' without telling the 6 substories in the process (which may each have varying degrees of relevance to main story you have to tell), this may be an area for support for you.

The trickiest part to this? If ADHD is also thrown in the mix – and the probability is very high, since at least 40% of autistic people also have ADHD – it'll be all too easy to constantly get side-tracked along the way of telling the 6 substories, in hopes that they'll piece into the one main story we really need to tell. Chances are, we might completely lose our way at some point and might feel that we need to start over again because we're confused which bits we've covered and which bits we haven't.

Socio-emotional expression (under 'Social cues' -> 'Output')

Most people would already be aware of the tendency for autistic people to struggle with picking up social cues (the 'social cues input' bit on the mind map), so we're not going to go into that. Instead, we'll discuss the lesser-known differences in the 'output', i.e., differences in any autistic person's use of their own facial expressions, body language and tone of voice. We briefly touched on society's misconception about eye contact, but let's unpack it some more. If anyone's ever asking about the *absence* or *presence* of eye contact in the context of autism, they're asking the wrong question.

Let's put it this way: Regardless of our neurotype, when we're having an enjoyable exchange with another person, we don't ask ourselves, "Is there eye contact happening??" More accurately, eye contact doesn't even usually cross our minds at all. Not ours, not the other person's. This generally happens when the interaction is happening with someone who shares the same neurotype we have, or with someone whom we know is a safe person, even if they have a different neurotype because they don't judge our differences.

However, when the interaction is with a NT who may have little awareness, understanding or acceptance of neurodivergence, differences in the use of eye contact may be picked up. Lack of eye contact may be interpreted as a lack of sincerity, confidence or respect. Too much eye contact (e.g., semi-staring as a compensatory behaviour) may be interpreted as being creepy or intimidating.

For most NTs, this all comes instinctively – when to look (at the other person), how long to look, when to look away, when to look again. And not all autistic people struggle with eye contact necessarily. Some may not struggle at all, some may be able to do it but feel uncomfortable, some may struggle with flexibly incorporating it into their communication, some may struggle with it intensely. Therefore, asking whether or not eye contact is present is really only scratching the surface.

Tone of voice, facial expressions and gestures may be another area of 'output' difference. Some autistic people have naturally flat affect (emotional expression, more specifically), which means they might have a flatter tone of voice, and less changes in facial expressions and use of gestures. It should be noted that a flatter emotional expression doesn't usually mean a lack of emotional experience. It just means that on the outside, there may be much less cues presented by the autistic person for others to pick up on what they might be feeling at any given time, unless their emotional experience is at a more extreme level.

Nevertheless, there are also autistic people who are on the other end of the 'output' spectrum, who are very expressive, flamboyant or animated in their expression. They might frequently make big gestures, have a lot of variation in their tone of voice, like a good storyteller would, and use a lot of lively facial expressions. There are also a lot of autistic people who have a somewhat average 'output' overall, not dissimilar to that of NTs.

Executive functioning

Executive functioning (EF) is basically a bunch of important skills across multiple areas that our brains engage in to help us make decisions, plan for the future, and do things with a purpose to steadily achieve our goals. There is more general awareness around the connection between executive dysfunction and ADHD, compared to autism, even though it's also one of the main areas of difficulty for autistic folks. On our autism mind map, an area of EF in particular, which describes the flexibility of a person's thinking and

© Jasmine Loo Psychology 2023

behaviours, was specified. This should be unsurprising, considering the general aversion (albeit to varying degrees) amongst most autistic people to surprises, uncertainties and the great unknown.

Challenges in this area can really affect how a person function in their daily life. They may show up as difficulties to switch from one task to another in a timely manner, or from one 'mode' of being to another (e.g., work-to-rest mode, rest-to-work mode, 'disciplining parent mode' to 'care-providing parent mode' and vice versa, etc). It can even have implications on psychotherapy - if someone who struggles with this area is getting help from a mental health professional, it might take them longer to see progress in therapy. Those (both NDs and therapists) who aren't aware of this might misinterpret the slow progress as therapy 'not working' and give up on it all too soon.

Facing challenges in this EF area isn't just about how you act; it can also affect how you feel. Life is always throwing new things at us, which can be very overwhelming even for those who don't struggle with this area of EF, let alone those who do. For NDs with extreme difficulties in this area of EF, it can create a vicious cycle where they struggle to implement the necessary changes that can make things better, and the stress resulting from that makes their EF struggles even worse.

If you can relate to feeling stuck in this cycle and it's causing a lot of distress, you could consider talking to a psychiatrist about the possibility of getting assessed for ADHD alongside your autism. This doesn't mean your autism diagnosis is wrong or invalid. Unlike autism, there are treatments available for ADHD. Medication, under proper medical guidance, has been shown by research to help about 70-80% of ADHDers. For some NDs who really struggle with this aspect of EF, ADHD medication can give them a break from this vicious cycle, improving their ability to handle changes.

Nevertheless, the autism mind map's specification of this EF domain doesn't imply that it's the only area of EF impacted for autistic people. Rather, this is because it tends to be the EF domain that's most consistently demonstrated in our research literature to be a struggle amongst autistic individuals. Some autistic people may have challenges across many more, or even all EF domains. We'll be diving into the rest of the EF domains in Chap. 2, when we look at ADHD. The autism research findings tend to be a bit more of a mixed bag when it comes to other EF domains, an occurrence not uncommon in neurodivergence research.

While it can be frustrating when science doesn't offer us clear-cut answers, if you remember our discussions on the heterogeneity of neurodivergence, it'd make much more sense to have inconsistent findings, even when the studies are robust in their methodologies. After all, we (well, most of us) would never go around making claims like, "All women can't drive", why should we expect to be able to say, "All autistic people are bad at XYZ", or conversely, "All autistic people are great at ABC"?

Emotional experience

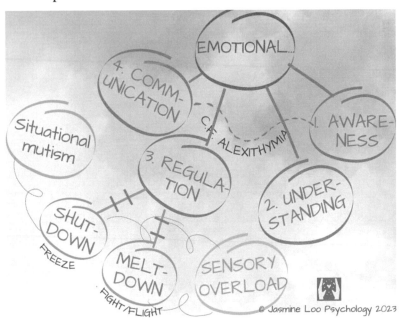

© Jasmine Loo Psychology 2023

This is an incredibly interesting area that not many are aware of, especially around the topic of alexithymia. We cannot truly understand the ND emotional processing, and figure out how to support or improve the mental health of NDs without fully grasping all of this. However, since all of this will be unpacked in Chap. 7 where we dive into the topic of ND emotional experiences and mental health, we won't be going into it here. So, stay tuned!

Sensory processing differences

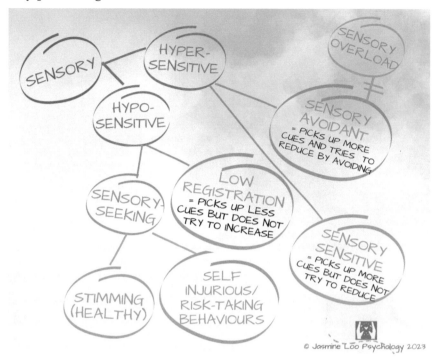

© Jasmine Loo Psychology 2023

    Since sensory modulation (or sensory regulation) struggles are an area that also affects ADHD-ers, we'll be discussing it in Chap. 2 instead because wouldn't we all get a bit sick of an overly long chapter? *Is there anything in this chapter that you really relate to?* _____

_____

_____

_____

_____

_____

Is there anything on the autism mind map that you identify as your strength(s)?

_____

_____

_____

_____

_____

2.

FACES OF ADHD

Understanding ADHD Beyond the DSM-5-TR

O K, I know that in Chap. 1 on autism, I talked about the amount of research work that goes into fine-tuning something like the DSM criteria. But when we look at what we've got on ADHD so far, nothing truly makes much sense – from its diagnostic criteria down to its name. If you're thinking, "Why is this book still calling it ADHD, then?", well, we've got to call it *something*. How else are we going to talk about it at all now? First off, take a look at the DSM-5-TR ADHD diagnostic criteria on the next page. If you thought, "Wow, that's a lot of words", you're not alone. ADHD diagnostic reports are always fun to write.

Essentially, based on the current ADHD diagnostic criteria, an ADHDer can either be diagnosed with ADHD - Predominantly inattentive presentation, or ADHD – Predominantly hyperactive-impulsive presentation, or ADHD – Combined presentation (i.e., hitting the jackpot with both types of ADHD presentations).

While this differentiation using subtypes helps with the awareness and acknowledgement of the existence of ADHDers who don't present with overt hyperactivity, it does make you wonder about the practical function it serves, since the treatment for ADHD does not differ based on the different subtypes. And the neurological underpinnings of the different subtypes are basically the

(Continue reading after diagram)

Attention-Deficit/Hyperactivity Disorder (ADHD)
DSM-5-TR diagnostic criteria

Reference: American Psychiatric Association. (2022). Neurodevelopmental disorders. In Diagnostic and statistical manual of mental disorders (5th ed., text rev.).

I. Chronic difficulties (i.e., $\geq$ 6 months) that are inconsistent with overall developmental level in the area(s) of:

INATTENTION (at least 5 of the following, if $\geq$ 17 years old): **AND / OR**

- Frequently makes careless mistakes or overlooks details in tasks/activities.
- Often struggles to maintain attention, e.g., throughout an exam, or a movie.
- Often appears distracted when directly spoken to, even without any apparent distractors.
- Frequent struggles adhering to instructions and completing tasks, e.g., may have semi-completed projects
- Tends to have poor organisation, e.g., double-booking appointments, being late, missing deadlines
- Averse to, or often avoids tasks demanding long periods of continuous focus, e.g., filling out lengthy forms
- Frequently misplaces items required for tasks/ activities (e.g., school/ work supplies and tools, personal belongings).
- Focus is often affected by external distractions, e.g., sounds from passing traffic, or by own thoughts.
- Frequently forgets important daily activities (e.g., chores, replying to emails , paying bills).

HYPERACTIVITY-IMPULSIVITY (at least 5 of the following, if $\geq$ 17 years old):

- Frequently moves hands or feet restlessly or fidgets while seated.
- Frequently gets up from their seat in situations where there is an expectation to stay seated (e.g., in class, the office, the theatre).
- Frequently engaging in untimely running or climbing; however in adolescents and adults, it may only manifest in the form of restlessness.
- Frequently has difficulty playing or participating in leisure activities in a quiet manner.
- Appears to be constantly on the move, as if being powered by a motor. Others may find it effortful to keep up with them, e.g., finding it challenging or uncomfortable to stay still for long periods in restaurants or during meetings.
- Often engages in excessive talking.
- Frequently interrupts prematurely before others finish a question or sentence, e.g., finishing others' sentences, impatient with turn-taking in conversations.
- Frequently struggles to wait for their turn, e.g., in queues.
- Frequently interrupting or space-invading, e.g., intruding into conversations or games, using others' belongings without permission. Adolescents and adults struggling with this may interfere with and take over what others are doing.

2. Experience of at least a few of the inattentive or hyperactive-impulsive symptoms before the age of 12.

3. Multiple symptoms of inattention or hyperactivity-impulsivity are noticeable across at least two different contexts relevant to the person's life, e.g., home, school, friendships, leisure.

4. Symptoms significantly hinder a person's engagement in one or more major life domains (e.g., social, vocational/educational, emotional).

5. These symptoms cannot be fully accounted for by schizophrenia, other psychotic disorders, or other mental disorders, e.g., depression, anxiety, personality disorder, substance intoxication or withdrawal.

Specification of either: Predominantly inattentive presentation, OR Predominantly hyperactive-impulsive presentation, OR Combined presentation same, just different manifestations of symptoms. This is because like autism, ADHD is a heterogenous condition (refer to Chap. 1 for definition). Imagine if the best practice recommendations for autism diagnoses follows the same logic, we'll end up with a gazillion autism diagnostic subtypes. It's kind of like, we may all get very hungry at some point. How that experience of hunger presents for different people might be different, however.

Some people tend to get 'hangry'. Some people tend to feel dizzy. Some people tend to start getting gastric pains. The physiological process driving these different manifestations of hunger are the same: the body's need for (and lack of) food. You address them in the same way: eat. And so, number of words aside, the attempt to describe ADHD still feels rather... hollow. Many of the sub-criteria sounded like a repetition of another sub-criterion describing essentially the same thing but in a different context.

I mean, it did demonstrate all the different ways one could explain the qualities of being "forgetful", "distractable" and "hyperactive". But it doesn't tell us much about what ADHD truly is. It's therefore important for us to look much deeper into ADHD, and beyond the clinical model for a more well-rounded understanding of it. *By simply looking at the DSM-5-TR criteria, how much do you think your presentation and experience fit or not fit the descriptions?*

_____

_____

_____

_____

First Things First

The very first thing you should know about ADHD, if you haven't already, is that ADHD is **not** the lack of focus and attention, but the **dysregulation** of focus and attention. This is why it's unsurprising find young ADHDers glued to screens for ages. It doesn't mean their ADHD diagnoses aren't valid because "they can focus then", but that they struggle to *flexibly shift* their focus onto other things that need their focus and attention.

And this dysregulation is primarily tied to 2 of the many naturally present brain chemicals (science speak: "neurotransmitters") for humans, called dopamine and norepinephrine (also called noradrenaline). Think of dopamine as a reward signal or a 'feel-good' chemical in your brain that's released when you do something enjoyable or accomplish a goal.

The reward system of your brain uses dopamine to let you know, "Hey, that was great! Keep doing it!" Once again, this is not a neurochemistry textbook, but to put it simply, the main driving factors of the presentations and challenges that ADHDers experience are found to be linked to reduced dopamine activities (in addition to dopamine not working how it's supposed to), and differences in the brain's reward system.

Because neuroscientists have been able to track ADHD back to its roots involving these brain chemicals, the current first line treatment recommendation for ADHD is psychostimulant medications, and non-stimulant medications being the second line treatment (i.e., next best treatment option, if the first line treatments don't work, or aren't suitable for you for any reason). Basically, psychostimulants work by helping the brain make and/or keep more norepinephrine, and non-stimulants work by slowing down the speed that norepinephrine is broken down in our system.

Once these brain chemical levels are where it should be (like how it's like for most NT brains), the brain can then function without needing to constantly be on the lookout for 'dopamine-mining' behaviours (a current popular slang word amongst ADHDers to mean behaviours that give the brain a rush of dopamine) to launch into. To the ADHD brain, consciously or unconsciously so, finding dopamine-mining things is like a Niffler finding shiny objects. If you aren't well-versed in Harry Potter, Nifflers are magical creatures in Potterverse that *love* anything with bling and will go nuts at the slightest glimpse of it. Once the medication or dopamine-rush wears off, however, the brain chemical level becomes out of whack again, leading to more ADHD struggles once more.

Legal stimulants (e.g., nicotine and caffeine), depressants that have stimulating effects (e.g., alcohol and opiates), as well as risky or extreme behaviours (e.g., high-risk sex, pornography, being in volatile relationships, gambling, fast driving, excessive overworking and compulsive spending) are some examples of unhealthy dopamine-mining methods. Well, coffee is exempted; us Melbournians take great pride in our coffee.

Jokes aside, it makes sense why addiction, in one form or another, is one of the most common co-occurring conditions for ADHD (no, it doesn't mean every ADHDer experiences addiction). Understanding the inner workings of an ADHD brain is an important first step in assessing the health and sustainability of our lifestyle and relationships. This is partly the reason why the health of ND relationships is one of the first topics in this book (Chap. 4).

A very regular concern that parents have about medicating their ADHD children is that they would "cause" their children to develop an addiction. But prescription psychostimulants under the guidance and monitoring of a medical professional are planets away from illicit stimulants off the streets. In fact, research shows that medication treatment of ADHDers significantly *reduces* the risks of self-medicating and developing addiction problems down the road.

One of the prejudices held against ADHD that's arguably the most hurtful is when ADHD (especially when unmedicated) is seen as a moral deficit. It's like if we were to put a fish at the base of a tree and expecting it to go up the tree like a monkey would, then make a moral judgment on the fish for failing and just flapping and gasping for air. If you never had access to support, and have times where you wonder how you could know for sure if the problem wasn't actually just you, ADHDers, *you deserve support*. You deserve to be the fish that gets to stay in the water. Seek out support. Nonetheless, getting medicated is only one part of the picture, self-understanding is also crucial. Like Chap. 1, we'll be discussing different aspects of ADHD using the mind map on the next page. Each cluster of the ADHD experience is represented by a unique colour to help with locating it on the main mind map. Let's take a look at it.

ADHD

Executive Functioning
- Burn-out
- Procras-tination
- Self-observing
- Initiation
- Working memory
- Task monitor
- Emotional regulation
- Shift/Transition
- Relationship struggles
- Irrelevant cues
- Inhibit
- Impulses
- Motivation
- Plan/Organise
- Order of environment

MASKING

Activity levels
- Average
- High
- Low
- Fidget
- Restless
- Interrupts
- Hyper-active
- Sleep issues

- Risk-taking behaviours/interests
- ↑ risk of accidental injury
- May have a lot to say/share
- Sensory-Seeking & Low Registration
- Trouble relaxing always feel the need to be doing something

Language & communication
- Receptive
- Expressive
- Gifted-ness
- Listening/understanding instructions
- Learning difficulties

Twice-exceptional

Cognitive differences
- Sluggish cognitive tempo (hypo-active)
- Process-ing speed
- Memory
  - Long-term memory (retrieval)
  - Working memory Low → High
  - Word-Finding difficulty

Emotions
- Heightened intensity & sensitivity
- Alexi-thymia
- Rejection sensitivity dysphoria (RSD)
- Pathological demand avoidance (PDA)
- Melt-down
- Shut-down FREEZE · FIGHT/FLIGHT

Sensory
- Sensory-seeking
- HYPO-sensitive
  - Low Registration
- HYPER-sensitive
  - Sensory Sensitive
  - Sensory Avoidant
  - Sensory Overload

Focus & Attention
- Hyper-focusing on current interests
- Distract-ability
- Forget-fulness
- Careless-ness
- Staying on task
- Task persist-ence

R.I.P. Past special interests & abandoned projects

Temporal Myopia = more focused on the immediate present, instead of info. related to the past or future.
- Time Perception differences

© Jasmine Loo Psychology 2023

31

Unpacking the ADHD Mind Map

ADHD masking: An overkill of compensation strategies

The title of this subsection probably says it all when it comes to ADHD masking. And it's not an exaggeration. Not sure where that's coming from? Let's see... Tend to not notice the time and run late for appointments? Set 10 alarms or reminders to go off at 5-minute intervals. Tend to have trouble getting started with work or study again once you allow yourself to rest and relax? Then don't relax! Milk every last bit of productivity while it lasts.

Tend to forget about a commitment if you were to start an activity a few hours before it? Then don't engage in any activities in all the hours before it! Sit and stare at the time with the lovely company of anxiety until it's time for what you committed to. Struggle staying seated and tend to annoy others who're very good at sitting still? Swap it with nail biting instead! Need I say more? For the record, these are only for illustrating common ADHD masking, and are NOT recommendations. Please don't do any of them.

Similar to autistic masking, ADHD masking tends to come hand in hand with bucket loads of anxiety. In fact, there's plenty of research findings showing the compensatory effect of anxiety for inhibition challenges amongst ADHDers. The irony is that, having too much anxiety can then further cripple our executive functioning (which we'll get into very soon), making ADHD symptoms even worse.

Most late-identified ADHDers go ages using these over-compensatory strategies without support and accommodation to look like they're not struggling, so that they could keep doing the everyday things that many may take for granted – work, life admin, socialising, maintaining relationships... The one area of life that tends to get neglected in order to pull all of this off is rest and relaxation.

People (ADHDers, health professionals, etc) tend to keep forgetting that ADHD is not something that just impacts work and study. It impacts *all* areas of life. Sadly though, when it comes to aspects of life that aren't generally observable for the outside world, such as having essential down-time, ADHDers tend to run out of fuel to adopt any strategies to nurture these parts of life. If you strongly relate to this, please stay tuned for Chap. 5, or reach out to a neuro-affirming mental health practitioner to start engaging in self-care that suits you.

Executive functioning, and focus and attention

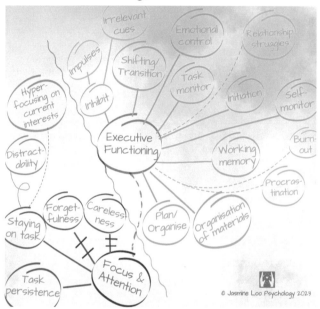

We discussed one particular aspect of executive functioning (EF) in Chap. 1. And it's almost impossible to understand ADHD without understanding EF. Given its significance, let's reiterate its definition. EF is basically a bunch of important and diverse skills that our brains engage in to help us make decisions, plan for the future, and do things with a purpose to systematically achieve our goals.

Oh, it's diverse alright, no kidding. Just look at how many areas it branches out to. These may seem like disjointed brain functions, but altogether, they're what helps us smoothly move through the things we need to do across the day. This unfortunately also explains why everything feels that much harder for ADHDers. We'll have trouble focusing on planning our day if we're feeling very dysregulated emotionally. We'll struggle to keep our surroundings tidy if we struggle with short-term memory.

The EF areas are all interconnected; but remember, the heterogeneity of

33

ADHD means that every ADHDer is going to be impacted in different EF areas to different degrees, forming unique EF profiles. We should remember that some NDs may not struggle at all, or might demonstrate a strength, in certain EF areas. Most EF research has been focused on EF challenges amongst NDs, but in 2020, there was a study that also investigated ND EF strengths. This area of research is still in its infancy stage, of course. The table below should help with clarifying what each area of EF means.

EF Area	Description of EF Area
Inhibit	The ease of resisting our own impulses, or engaging in unimportant external stimuli (distractibility), or in stopping one of our own behaviours at appropriate times.
Self-Observing	The ease of tapping into our own awareness of the possible effects that our actions may have on others (i.e., our social or interpersonal awareness).
Shift/ Transition	The ease of moving across different situations, activities, or aspects of a problem, as required by our changing circumstances.
Emotional Regulation	The ease of modulating our own emotional reactions/responses in different day-to-day situations.
Initiate	The ease of 'getting our engine started', getting started on a task or activity, and taking initiative in coming up with ideas, responses, or problem-solving strategies that can help with our daily functioning.
Working Memory	The ease of holding information in our minds just long enough to complete a specific task, or to simultaneously manipulate that information in our minds in ways to meet a certain purpose. Required for carrying out multi-step activities, completing mental manipulations (e.g., working out maths problems in our heads), and following multi-step instructions.
Plan & Organise	The ease of managing current and future-oriented task demands, including our ability to contemplate the likelihood

	of future events, bring order to all that information, set goals, and to develop suitable step-by-step plans in advance.
Task Monitor	The ease of keeping track of the success/failure of our problem-solving strategies, as well as of identifying and correcting any mistakes to improve success rate.
Order of Environment	The ease of keeping the orderliness of work, living, and storage spaces (e.g., desks, rooms).

Can you now see why the ADHD symptoms of "forgetfulness", "carelessness", "distractibility", etc are really underlying EF challenges? ND hyperfocusing has everything to do this, too – a combination of trouble resisting the urge to keep doing what we're doing (Inhibit) and shifting to another task we need to be doing (Shift/Transition). At times, working memory struggles also come into play, contributing to 'time-blindness', a lack of awareness of how much time has passed.

Unfortunately, if you thought your EF 'could not be worse', it absolutely could be – it's a dynamic capacity, which means that if we are tired or sick, or have been under stress for an extended period of time, our EF can absolutely take an even further dip. One of the many reasons why we should try to prevent ND burnout at all cost.

Sensory processing

The connection between sensory processing differences and autism has been well-documented in research, and is much more widely known amongst the general public, compared to that of ADHD and sensory processing differences. Sensory Processing Disorder and ADHD are 2 distinct conditions, but they commonly co-exist. Even though existing research is still primarily focused on children, there have been a small handful of studies on adult ADHDers recently, confirming differences in multiple areas within sensory processing, especially in sensory modulation (i.e., regulation).

Some ADHDers experiencing sensory processing challenges may only have one of the senses affected, some others may have multiple, if not all senses affected, but perhaps in different ways. To start, let's first have a look at our different senses. Most of us know the 5 human senses, but in fact, we have at least 8 senses, which are laid out in the diagram below:

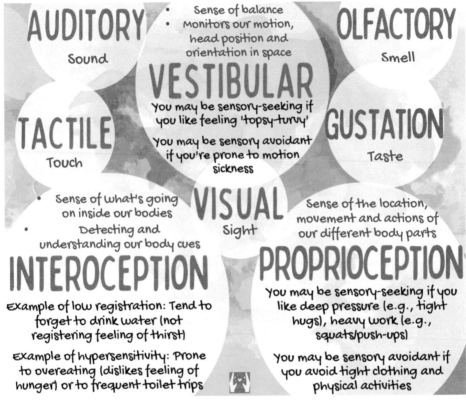

In addition to the examples on this infographic, interoception also has to do with our emotional awareness in real time. This is because we need to be able to pick up cues from our body, and put them together in a way that makes sense to link them to a particular emotional experience. Emerging research shows that ADHDers are at least twice as likely as non-ADHDers to have alexithymia (i.e., 'emotional blindness'), which will be discussed further in Chap. 7 on emotions and mental health.

Besides, it's also not uncommon for us see some young ADHDers who are vestibular sensory-seekers, and love zooming around, hanging upside down or doing cartwheels. Even though hyperactivity is generally shown to be toned down as we age (even to a level that's not noticeable by outsiders in adulthood for some), some adult ADHDers may cater to their vestibular sensory seeking by engaging in sports, such as surfing, roller-skating, mountain biking etc.

Proprioception is an interesting one – it's knowing exactly where our limbs and core are within the space around us, at all times. Our joints also have a lot of proprioceptive receptors, so that when we exert force on them, generally by exercising, we get more proprioceptive input than when our body's relaxed, or "all loose" (if simply reading those 2 words make you shudder, you know you're a sensory-seeker). It's always interesting to ask adult ADHDers how often their bodies feel relaxed (many would need further elaboration on what that means exactly).

It's relatively common to hear NDs reporting that their bodies are more frequently tensed up than not, which can cause regular aches and pains. Even though there hasn't been research looking specifically at effects of proprioceptive input on ADHDers' dopamine levels (not as far as I know of), we know that deep pressure stimulates the release of dopamine and serotonin. It's hence unsurprising that some ADHDers need to weave in regular exercise as part of their self-care routine.

Our jaws also have a lot of proprioceptive receptors, and so what can transpire for some ADHDers who are proprioceptive sensory-seeking is that they might almost constantly feel like munching something (usually crunchy or chewy foods, which gives the jaws a better workout). Binge-eating is another closely co-existing condition with ADHD partly due to this reason (it also triggers dopamine release because of the perceived rewards). For some others, it can also manifest into temporomandibular joint (TMJ) dysfunction, from consistent jaw clenching and teeth grinding. Most people are only aware of the absence/presence of outward hyperactivity in ADHDers, but may not realise that most ADHDers experience chronic internal restlessness and tension.

Now, onto what sensory modulation is all about… It's a subset of sensory processing, and involves differences in effectively 'tuning' the experience of the sensory experience up and down as we go along. Think of it as a bit like an editor of a TV show. Have you ever watched a TV show that's super frustrating, where the background music is super loud when the characters are literally talking, and you have to turn on the subtitles to know what they're saying?

Then, when there's no music, the characters' voices became way too soft and you have to turn the volume up, but the moment commercials start, you get what feels like a whiplash from how loud it is. Sensory modulating challenges are a bit like that. The diagram below explains the types of modulation differences:

HYPER-SENSITIVE
Naturally picks up more sensory stimuli than others/ has a lower threshold before registering sensory stimuli.

HYPO-SENSITIVE
Naturally picks up less sensory stimuli than others/ has a higher threshold before registering sensory stimuli.

SENSORY SENSITIVE
- Not bothered by hypersensitivity.
- Doesn't change behaviour to reduce stimulation.
  Presentation examples:
- Attend to irrelevant stimuli to an extent that it impacts on ability to focus on what they need to focus on.
- More distractible around intense stimuli.
- Have a high level of awareness of the environment.
- Can discriminate/ attend to detail.

SENSORY-AVOIDING
- Bothered & overwhelmed by stimuli.
- Actively engage with environments to reduce sensory stimuli.
  Presentation examples:
- Find their environments too intense or variable to function day-to-day.
- Able to create structure in environments that provide limited sensory stimuli.
- Show tolerance or enjoyment in being alone.

LOW REGISTRATION
- Not bothered by hyposensitivity.
- Doesn't change behaviour to increase stimulation.
  Presentation examples:
- Miss or take longer to respond to stimuli that others notice.
- Struggle reacting to rapidly presented or low-intensity stimuli.
- Not detect sensory stimuli that bother everyone else present.
- The last in the room to get a joke.
- Not respond when being called.

SENSORY-SEEKING
- Bothered by hyposensitivity.
- Create additional stimuli / look for environments that provide them.
  Presentation examples:
- Higher interests in exploring the environment.
- Regard sensory experiences as pleasurable.
- Become easily bored and may find low-stimulus environments intolerable.
- May involve risk-taking behaviours/ hyperactivity.

Our sensory profiles can really vary from person to person because this is yet another thing that's heterogenous. For instance, we might have low registration for our sense of smell and interoception, be sensory-seeking in our sense of proprioception and touch, sensory-sensitive in our sense of hearing, and sensory-avoidant in our sense of sight and vestibular input.

We're increasingly starting to understand the connections between sensory processing and emotions and mental health, especially in the context of neurodivergence. For example, it appears that there's a link between Low Registration and more severe depressive symptoms, as well as alexithymia, while Hypersensitivity (think sensory overload) is linked to increased anxiety. Oh, neurodivergence is one fun ride... sometimes.

Cognitive differences

Frustratingly, one of the commonly heard barriers that ADHDers face getting diagnosed is when clinicians think they're "too accomplished to have ADHD". It's a misconception that having ADHD must mean 'not as smart', or being unable to learn and work. Sure, many ADHDers struggle with study and work, but it's much more complex than just how smart they are, as this chapter has hopefully illustrated. Some ADHDers may be gifted or high-achieving. It doesn't mean they are immune to ADHD challenges, or that they don't have ADHD, though.

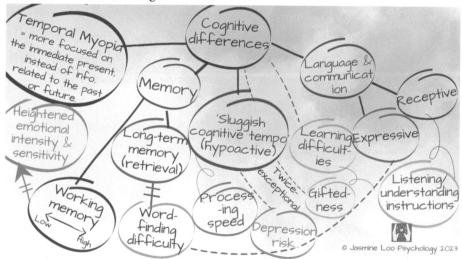

© Jasmine Loo Psychology 2023

Differences in sense of time

One of the neuro-cognitive differences that presents in ADHD is called "temporal myopia" (i.e., trouble with perception of time, or time orientation). ADHD challenges with perception of time have been backed by brain imaging and brain functioning research, and the degree of struggle directly corresponds with intensity of ADHD symptoms. This can have a widespread impact on the lives of ADHDers.

Here's an example: some of us might struggle to comprehend why we never seem to learn our lessons about something in particular. When we are in an annoying, or tricky situation, we might swear that we'll never ever do XYZ again. Fast forward to the next time we're in another similar situation, we may recall what happened and what we promised ourselves last time, and could imagine the possible consequences, but perhaps the immediate, short-term reward, whatever that may be, is still more appealing and attention-grabbing than the 'lesson' we somewhat remember. We might even repeat this cycle several times on the same thing.

Or it doesn't even have to be with a lesson we learnt – it could be about something we ourselves would consider 'common sense'. Delaying the gratification of having fun right now to study, so we can gain the future rewards of passing the subject, for instance. But even then, it can still be so hard. Temporal myopia can also give ADHDers the perception that more time has passed than it has in reality, making waiting feel more insufferable. This could be one of the explanations for increased impulsivity in ADHD. Other times, in social interactions, ADHDers may be under the impression that they've waited long enough before saying something, but to the other party, it may be seen as rude interjection.

Differences in memory function

Next on the list... memory. If we think of the brain as a computer, working memory (WM) would be the RAM, and long-term memory would be the hard drive of the computer. Even though many may think that ADHD is always linked to WM struggles, it's not as simple as that. Some ADHDers have average or even above average WM in terms of their cognitive ability. This may or may not always translate to WM in the executive functioning sense, however (as discussed previously).

To understand this, let's go back to the RAM analogy. If you're a techie, you'd be excited by the awesome specs of a new computer that's been released, and one of the appealing features may be a big RAM. But no matter how big the RAM of this new super computer may be, it's never going to be infinite. And if at any given time, you were to have 6 browser windows, 45 tabs on each of them, along with 79 PDFs and 56 Word windows up and running simultaneously, your big-RAM computer will still become slow and regularly become frozen (yes, start closing those tabs).

Aaaand we know that ND brains tend to be chronically busy brains, to put it mildly, which is kind of like this analogy. So, if you were to say open another Word document at this time, your computer might freeze or crash, even if it was previously running fine (somewhat). And you might get super frustrated at it, and think, "what kind of computer can't even handle running a WORD DOC???" Well, this is why. And emotional regulation is hardly a 'Word Doc'; it's more like trying to run Photoshop.

There's been more and more research on the link between WM challenges and emotional regulation for ADHDers. We're not imagining it – ADHDers do tend to experience emotions more intensely when they hit. Emotional regulation is a higher-order, complex brain function, instead of simply a matter of 'control' and willpower, as if it's something that can be achieved by exerting brute force over our emotions. In fact, doing that tends to backfire, which we'll explain in Chap 7.

When an event that occurs triggers an emotional reaction in us, we're essentially presented with at least a couple of different pieces of emotional information, *on top of* the different pieces of factual information about the event. That's a lot of pieces of information to hold and make sense of in our WM, a bit like in a sensory overload, we're hit by too many pieces of sensory information at the same time, and our computer becomes frozen.

When it comes to long-term memory (aka the 'hard drive'), there are 2 pathways to consider: storage and retrieval. Storage would be how easy we remember the new things we learn (transferring data to a hard disk drive that's using USB 3.0 is going to be much faster than one that has USB 2.0). Retrieval means how efficiently we can grab the stuff that has already previously been stored in our long-term memory to be used when we need it.

If you tend to speak in sentences that sound a bit like this (e.g., "You know, the...the thing that happened the other day... Will you call... um that guy and tell him about it?") because you struggle to 'conjure' the right words you needed and the person you're talking to would look at you with a face that says "What on earth are you talking about?" – that's your long-term memory retrieval. If you tend to speak half a sentence and forget the next half, then proceed to forget about what the first half was about, too, that's your WM. And yes, these examples made it into this book because they're not uncommon for ADHDers!

Most people would have times when they have thoughts that someone doesn't like them, or wish to spend time with them. But quickly, they might then tell themselves that there were plenty other times when that was proven untrue and start feeling better or move on with their day. However, many ADHDers have experienced different degrees of peer rejection across our lifetime, and long-term memory retrieval challenges can mean that the speed at which we could recover relevant pieces of memory that prove that to be untrue would be slower. Which means we gain some nice extra seconds or minutes where our mind gets flooded by many pieces of emotional information.

As above, WM struggles mean that we then get overloaded. This is likely why the term "rejection sensitivity dysphoria" (RSD) was coined even though there hasn't been much research done on it yet. Because of the number of ADHDers who find it relatable, it's included in the emotional cluster on the ADHD mind map in the next section.

Sluggish cognitive tempo (SCT)

'Sluggish cognitive tempo' (SCT) is yet another area closely related to neurodivergence with a terrible name. It still made its way into the mind map because it's important to still understand what it's all about before someone can come up with a better name – function over form. In the last year, the SCT Work Group suggested a name change to Cognitive Disengagement Syndrome, which is arguably just as cringey, but if you were to see that term in the near future instead, they're referring to the same thing. Most of the SCT research thus far links it to ADHD, but there's emerging research showing that it could be even more common amongst autistic people, especially AuDHDers (finally, ADHD had more research funding for a change).

There are 2 main parts to SCT: cognitive disengagement (e.g., daydreaming, frequent blank stares, losing train of thought, forgetting what they were going to say, easily confused) and hypoactivity, or slower motor movements (e.g., low activity level, easily tired, drowsy/sleepy during the day). According to the Work Group's 2023 large-scale study, cognitive disengagement symptoms are much more prevalent that hypoactive symptoms in ASD and ADHD-C (i.e., ADHD Combined Presentation) children, but roughly the same level across both areas for those with ADHD-I. Compared to 7% of NT children found with SCT on average, 32% of autistic children, 27% of ADHD-I children and 18% of ADHD-C children were found to present with SCT.

Other research found that SCT is connected to slower processing speed in completing tasks that require hand-eye coordination, lower memory performance (for co-existing ADHD x SCT), as well as lower likelihood of 'explosive' emotional struggles (e.g., aggressive meltdowns) but much higher likelihood of 'implosive' emotional struggles (e.g., depression, social withdrawal). This means that in addition to implications for learning difficulties, more importantly, SCT represents a major risk to developing depression – a link that extends into adulthood.

This is important to know because most people only think of hyperactivity when they hear 'ADHD', some may know that not all ADHDers present with hyperactivity, but very few would be aware that ADHD could also manifest as *underactivity*. If this resonates with you and you're experiencing depression (or suspect you may be), please seek support from a mental health professional. It's untrue that the only way we can go about improving mental health is by eliminating our risk factors because we don't necessarily have control over many of them – a healthy alternative is to build upon our protective factors (e.g., engaging in regular therapy, maintaining a support network and a reasonably healthy lifestyle, etc).

Emotional experience

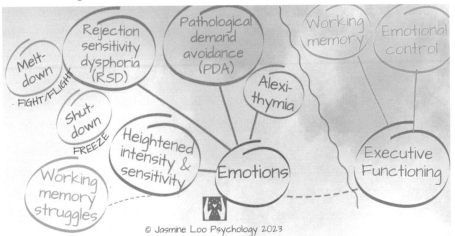

© Jasmine Loo Psychology 2023

There are a few concepts rather unique to the ADHD emotional experience. We briefly discussed in the last subsection one of the reasons why ADHDers tend to experience emotions in a much higher intensity, and hypotheses on how RSD came about. Many ADHDers have experienced long-term social setbacks and are no strangers to interpersonal rejection, which can also predispose us to be more concerned about, and feeling unsafe from rejection or potential rejection from others.

Alexithymia is one that appears to be shared by both autistic people and ADHDers, which will be covered in more detail in Chap. 7 of this book. Which leaves "pathological demand avoidance" (PDA). Personally, I'm not a big fan of the name, but it's what's it's commonly known by at this stage, so we'll go with that. Just like RSD, PDA isn't an official condition or presentation officially recognised in the current literature, and so hasn't got a lot of research on it. But it's also something relatable to many ADHDers.

PDA is really not all that hard to understand, even though people who don't understand it may be baffled by the degree of an ADHDer's reaction to a demand (or perceived demand) placed on them. Imagine if you can barely walk across the room without tripping over or knocking something over (not so hard for many of us to imagine that), and someone tells you that you have to ski down a steep and snowy mountain. Um... anyone in that situation would freak out?

Most ADHDers are highly anxious one way or another because of difficulties we experience, even in tasks that NTs without EF challenges may find so easy and automatic, they don't even think about it. It'd be a massive relief if we manage to somewhat manage the day. Any additional (objective or subjective) demands may just be enough to tip us over the edge, and into a meltdown or shutdown. Being in a supportive and understanding environment (Chap. 4), good self- and emotional understanding (Chaps. 3, 7 and 8), as well as regular self-care (Chap. 5) are some of the key things that can help us surf the waves of different emotions.

At last...

Now that we looked at the different main aspects of ADHD throughout this chapter, don't all the different DSM characteristics naturally fall into their own places where they make sense? *Is there anything in this chapter that you really relate to?*_____

_____

_____

_____

_____

Is there anything on the ADHD mind map that you identify as your strength?

_____

_____

_____

_____

SECTION II

UNDERSTANDING *MY* NEURODIVERGENCE

&

LATE-IDENTIFICATION

3.

UNPACKING MY NEURODIVERGENT JOURNEY

I n the previous chapters in Section I, we delved into autism and ADHD beyond the clinical model based on the DSM-5-TR diagnostic criteria. Did it match how you understood autism and ADHD before starting this book? Or were there things you didn't know before, but can relate to? This chapter, we're going to start discussing late-identification of neurodivergence specifically and to reflect on what it means to you.

At what age did you find out you were neurodivergent (ND)? _____

What It Means to Be a Late-Identified Neurodivergent Adult

Historically, ASD and ADHD research (or any research, really) was often being led by researchers who are white academic, neurotypical males, with study participants mostly from a similar demographic, creating biases in research findings. These findings were then used to inform the creation of formal diagnostic criteria, leading to inaccurate gender ratios for ASD and ADHD.

For instance, the documented male to female ratio for autistic people of 4:1 is now believed to be closer to 2:1. Interestingly, the earliest autism research study in 1943 had 11 autistic participants, 3 of whom were girls. Similarly, the earliest ADHD research study had 15 male and 5 female participants, and the current documented male to female ratio is 3:1. The methods used and conclusions drawn do leave one wondering if they understood the ratio formula in math class. The gender bias in research continues for decades after the earliest studies found.

These biases extend beyond empirical research. Much of society's misconception about autism stems from the direct conjuring of an image of someone who is white, male, and generally a child (news break, ND children grow into ND adults). And when they hear ADHD, they think of a (generally male) child who's bouncing off the walls. Research shows that boys have a higher likelihood than girls to be overt and show more disruptive behaviours in class, whereas girls generally exhibit more cognitive and academic struggles. Because of this, undisruptive girls are more likely to go unnoticed.

Similarly, even many of those who are aware of autism in adults still think of Sheldon from Big Bang Theory or Rain Man. This is not to imply that there's anything wrong with NDs who present that way, but that it's important to acknowledge that these are by no means the only faces of autism and ADHD. Write some factors that you believe contributed to your late-identification below.

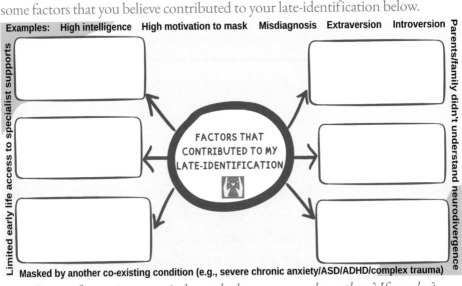

Examples: High intelligence   High motivation to mask   Misdiagnosis   Extraversion   Introversion

Parents/family didn't understand neurodivergence

Limited early life access to specialist supports

FACTORS THAT CONTRIBUTED TO MY LATE-IDENTIFICATION

Masked by another co-existing condition (e.g., severe chronic anxiety/ASD/ADHD/complex trauma)

Do any factors in your mind map bother you more than others? If so, why?

(Continue on the next page)

Generally, late-identified NDs are ones who deviate from these stereotypical ND presentations, and missed early identification and targeted supports through their formative years. This can have a profound impact on their psychological wellbeing. They may have been called many hurtful names, such as 'lazy', 'volatile', 'not a good team player', 'weird', etc. It often leaves people feeling broken, as if something was wrong with them, when in fact, they're just different. Had this been your experience? If so, fill out the diagram below.

Many adults start seeking clarification and learning about neurodivergence only when they encounter life crises, usually when increased life demands exceeded their coping capacities. Finding out they're ND helps many look at themselves and the lives they've lived from a different angle. For many, it can be the starting point of a journey towards self-understanding and acceptance.

I'm Male/Non-Binary but Relate to the 'Female Presentation'

The ND discourse and landscape is ever-changing because every day, we are gaining better understanding and insight through consistent streams of new research findings, conversations within the ND communities, advocacy, etc. Even though females have historically been seriously underdiagnosed, there isn't

49

a gendered presentation of neurodivergence per se.

The notion of a female presentation refers to NDs who are highly motivated to 'mask' and 'camouflage', i.e., to act in ways seen as socially acceptable or neurotypical (NT), often driven by the need to ensure personal safety and conditional social acceptance. Females are also much more likely to be misdiagnosed or have a delayed diagnosis compared to males because of the high likelihood of masking. Heavy masking amongst NDs have been shown to be linked to higher clinical anxiety and depression.

However, it isn't exclusively females who engage in masking – some men, trans men who were socialised as women, and nonbinary people may also share this presentation. Perhaps then, a more accurate term may be an atypical presentation of neurodivergence. *What do you think? What would you call it?*_____

_____

For some adults who went through formal assessments, the journey can be confusing, challenging and frustrating, to say the least. Long waitlists, health professionals being unfamiliar with atypical ND presentations, self-doubt, discouragement from close circle are some examples of the many challenges that people often face. *Did you face any challenges with the assessment process? If self-identified, did you face any personal / social challenges in identifying as ND?*

_____

_____

_____

_____

_____

The whole process of identification, formal or informal, can be an emotional roller coaster, even after it is 'over'. Some of the emotions that surface in this process may be expected, others may be unexpected. And you might feel differently about your neurodivergence on different days (perhaps even different moments) - sometimes how you feel about it one day may be the complete opposite of how you feel about it on another day. All of this is normal and OK.

Now, write some emotion words that describe how you've been feeling since discovering you're ND on the mind map below. If you'd like some example words, have a look at the table at the bottom. As you work through this book, you might find that you'd like to add in more emotion words, or if you prefer to do this activity later on instead – that's fine. Building insight isn't a linear process!

Pleasant Emotion Words		Unpleasant Emotion Words	
High Energy	Low Energy	High Energy	Low Energy
Excited	Relieved	Anxiety	Grief
Happy	Peace	Anger	Sadness
Empowered	Calm	Aggrieved	Mournful
Confident	Belongingness		Uncertainty

Viewing Myself Through Neurodivergent Lenses

Finding out you're ND doesn't change who you are, or your past, nor does it guarantee that your future will be one way or another. But hopefully, by reframing your life story through ND lenses, you could feel a bit more self-compassion and start treating yourself with more gentleness from here on. To develop a healthier self-view, it's important to equally acknowledge both our strengths and difficulties (news break: everyone has both!). Being ND just means being different, not less or defective. You might like the analogy of comparing a Windows operating system with a Mac operating system (in comparing NTs with NDs). Both of these operating systems have their own

strengths and shortcomings, but we wouldn't generally say one is 'less than' the other, much less say that one of them is 'wrong' or 'defective'.

In fact, it can be more of an issue if you thought you have a Windows OS the entire time and keep trying to install and run Windows compatible programs, when in fact you have a Mac OS. Of course, you'd be ripping your hair out wondering why it's not working and why everything is so hard. Acknowledging our strengths help us tap into our existing tools and resources to meet life's challenges, and possibly even to support our areas of difficulty. So, try and see if you could identify and write *your top 3 ND strengths and difficulties* below:

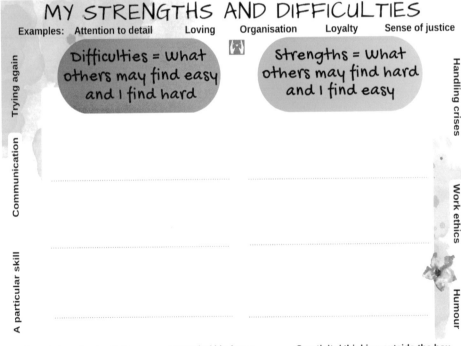

MY STRENGTHS AND DIFFICULTIES

Examples: Attention to detail   Loving   Organisation   Loyalty   Sense of justice

Difficulties = what others may find easy and I find hard

Strengths = what others may find hard and I find easy

Trying again

Communication

A particular skill

Handling crises

Work ethics

Humour

Knowledge about a topic   Empathy/ kindness   Creativity/ thinking outside the box

Timeline Activity: Plot 2 challenging events that you've experienced in your life prior to your ND diagnosis/identification in the space under the line (marked '-'), and 2 instances in your life when you had felt good about yourself in the space above the line that's marked '+' (e.g., when you had an achievement, when you feel proud or at peace with a decision you made/how you handled something).

Please note that the challenging moments don't have to be life adversities, especially if using them for this exercise may be too triggering for you (if so, they may be more suitable to be worked on in therapy with your psychologist). The 4 timeline events also don't need to be 'caused by'/related to your neurodivergence; they can be any events you find suitable that fit the above description.

Plot the events in chronological order (i.e., the further right on the timeline, the more recent the event). Write no more than a few keywords for each. As long as you know what you're referring to when you look at it, that's enough. It doesn't have to make sense for anyone else.

+

-

3. UNPACKING MY ND JOURNEY

Now, I'd like you to imagine putting on a pair of glasses with special lenses – neurodivergent lenses – and looking back at your experience of these 4 events now that you know you're neurodivergent (and always have been, even when you didn't know it), what do you make of these experiences? You can use the prompts below to help with your reflections. Remember to refer to the contact list of your support network on pg. 6, if you need some support with this exercise.

If you enjoy writing and need more space than the lines provided, please write or type your reflections on a separate document. If you don't, consider writing using the voice-to-text function on Google Docs (or similar apps) to jot down your reflections. Instructions can be found here: https://support.google.com/docs/answer/4492226?hl=en#zippy=%2Ctype-with-your-voice

Self-reflection question prompts:

1. Do you see these events, or see yourself in that point in time, any differently than how you used to, before you realised you were neurodivergent?

1a. If so, what are the differences – seeing them with and without ND lenses?

_____

_____

_____

_____

_____

_____

_____

*2. Now, imagine this timeline was experienced by a loved one (e.g., your child, close friend, partner, or a dearly beloved fictional character) whom you did not previously know was ND. Put on your ND lenses again. What would you say to them? What sentiments would you share about the highs and lows of their lives?*_____

_____

_____

_____

  (Continue on the next page)

_____

_____

_____

_____

*2a. Is your response for Question 2 any different from your personal reflections from 1a? If so, how are they different?*_____

_____

_____

_____

_____

_____

*2b. Why do you think they're different?*_____

_____

_____

_____

_____

_____

Nothing and no one can change the objective facts about what happened in the past, but our subjective view and understanding of past events can have major impacts on not only how we feel about them, but also how we might see and feel about ourselves. When we don't have a choice but to operate in ways that we aren't wired to, day after day, it makes sense for it to be extra challenging.

Conversely, when we put on our neurodivergent lenses, any personal achievements and progress that we may have taken for granted, perhaps because we couldn't help but compare them to others' achievements, may be a bigger deal than we gave them credit for. We've covered a lot in a single chapter and you might feel a wave of tiredness later on, just like our muscles might ache after a good workout. So, remember to make time to rest and recuperate, and to go easy on yourself. Go through this book at a pace you're comfortable with; there's no rush.

4.

NEURODIVERGENT RELATIONSHIP HEALTH

[Trigger alert: Discussions of interpersonal abuse in this chapter]

This chapter, we'll be looking into some important things that can affect the health of (any of) our relationships. For many NDs (NTs, too, really), having good role models for building and maintaining healthy relationships may be a privilege that was sadly not being extended to them while growing up. This can make an already challenging life skill even harder. If this is an area for development for you, unpacking the fundamentals of healthy and unhealthy relationships today can be a good start. But first, let's do a quick review of what we covered last chapter:

- Some possible reasons for late-identification of neurodivergence.
- Explored what your neurodivergence meant for you, and what your emotional journey since identification has been like.
- Reflecting on not only your challenges, but also your strengths.

Power Dynamics in Relationships

Power dynamics in relationships refers to ways of interacting that influence the other party's behaviour – but it isn't always about dominance and submission. We tend to shy away from the word (and the entire concept of) 'power' when it comes to authentic personal relationships, as if power was a dirty word. However, it's inevitable for us as humans to influence each other. You see, each party in a relationship will present with a unique package of qualities (e.g., core beliefs, needs, values, personality, world view). No two people in the world will present with the exact same package. This means that not only would it be impossible to find another human being who's identical to us in how we resolve problems that surface in a relationship, it's impossible to find someone identical to us even in the way we *look at* the problems. And in the negotiation process to reach a state of harmony and balance in the relationship, power dynamics come into existence. For this reason, power dynamics will always be at play in every relationship.

We can be the role model we needed as children for ourselves

Having said that, there are healthy and unhealthy power dynamics in relationships. When there's an imbalance of power, it can manifest in many different ways (e.g., resentment, endless arguments, and emotional distance). Having both parties in a relationship being mindful of the power dynamics of the relationship and working together on an ongoing basis to maintain a balanced power dynamic is essential for maintaining a healthy relationship.

Many might hold the misconception that healthy power dynamics are only important in, or relevant to intimate partner relationships, but that's not true. It's, in fact, essential for the health of relationships of any sort (e.g., romantic relationships, friendships, family and collegial relationships, etc.).

You can think of power dynamics between two parties in a relationship as two people on a seesaw. Now, it's probably been a while since any of us has been on a seesaw, but we could probably all recall what it was like to play on a seesaw with a mate when we were children. Check out the infographic on the next page for a visual prompt to help you conceptualise the seesaw analogy on power dynamics.

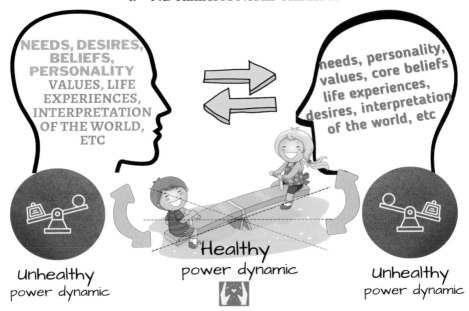

Healthy power dynamic

Unhealthy power dynamic   Unhealthy power dynamic

Healthy vs unhealthy power dynamics

Healthy power dynamics in a relationship can be like playing on a seesaw. Each party takes turns going up and down (i.e., listening and communicating/ giving and receiving/ leading and following/ asserting and compromising, etc in a relationship), allowing for the relationship to be fluid and dynamic. At times, both parties may need to communicate with each other to coordinate, so that you don't both push at the same time. Once you find your momentum, it's fun because both parties get a fair share of excitement from being up high and security from feet grounded to the earth.

Often, circumstances aren't ideal, and we can't have both parties' needs tended to simultaneously in a healthy relationship. Sometimes you will compromise for the other person's needs; other times, they take care of your needs. The mutually agreed upon rules in your relationship are honoured by *both* parties, so that it's mostly fair overall.

Occasionally, from the moment a relationship is established, power imbalance may already be present through no fault of either party. Perhaps it's due to a big difference in the levels of life or working experience between the two parties (i.e., the party with much more experience being in a position of power). Perhaps there's a big difference in income-generating capacity between a couple in a long-term relationship (i.e., the party with much more earning capacity being in a position of power in the financial aspect of the relationship, or beyond).

Automatic power imbalance could also be due to the nature of the relationship. Take a parent-child relationship, for example. Putting aside the differences in age and life experience, there will still be a natural power imbalance because parents are in the position to care for, be responsible for, set rules and boundaries (discipline) and teach their children.

This scenario is a bit like when we used to play on the seesaw with a mate who was twice our body weight, a situation which I'm sure most of us would have encountered at some point. In that case, whether it became a fun experience for us would depend on what our mate did. If they were simply slumped on their end of the seesaw without pushing, we'd be left with our little legs hanging mid-air, uncertain about how or when we could get off. But if they were to be aware of the imbalance from the get-go, and made sure that they pushed with an appropriate force and supported themselves using their tippy toes, so we had a chance to push, too, it could still be fun.

The analogy above can be applied to understanding contexts where there's a natural power imbalance from the get-go. The person with naturally more power in the relationship has to be the party to make sure they balance up the relationship's power dynamics. More specifically, you can say that they're the only party that's capable of truly making that happen.

Unhealthy relationship dynamics generally lack the sort of turn-taking/give-and-take we were talking about. One party's needs and wants often outweighs the other party's, and each person plays either the role of the giver or the taker without much interchange. On the rare occasion that they behave differently, it may be to serve an agenda that may or may not be immediately clear to the affected party, or to maintain 'the cycle of abuse' (which will be discussed in the next section).

Abuse, Relational Trauma and Neurodivergence

Research findings indicate that children with ASD and ADHD have significantly higher prevalence of exposure to neighbourhood violence, parental divorce, mental illness, substance abuse, and higher overall cumulative Adverse Childhood Experiences (ACE) scores, exceeding the established threshold of 4 ACEs, compared to those without ASD and ADHD. The higher the ACE score, the higher the risk for poor general outcomes, e.g., poor mental health, highlighting the importance of those at risk to seek professional support. [1]

Differences in the ways NDs understand the world can put us in a more vulnerable position in being subjected to abuse (some of which were covered in Chap. 1 and 2), even though there's hardly any sole reason or straightforward explanation as to why this is the case. Many NDs may not be aware that their experiences are considered abuse or unhealthy relationship patterns. Awareness is key, so let's unpack healthy, unhealthy and abusive relationships to break the veil. To start, think about some common elements or characteristics of toxic relationships and write them on the flags below.

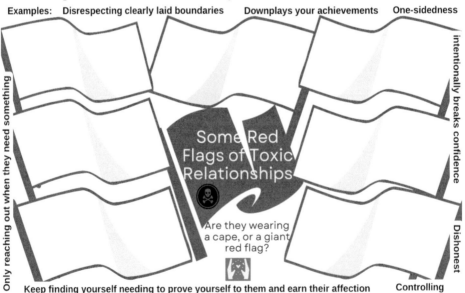

Examples: Disrespecting clearly laid boundaries   Downplays your achievements   One-sidedness

Only reaching out when they need something

intentionally breaks confidence

Some Red Flags of Toxic Relationships

Are they wearing a cape, or a giant red flag?

Dishonest

Keep finding yourself needing to prove yourself to them and earn their affection   Controlling

---

[1] For information on the original study on ACEs, including the most common categories of ACEs, visit https://www.cdc.gov/violenceprevention/aces/about.html#anchor_08037

Abuse is so much more than simply physical abuse. This is not to downplay the seriousness of physical abuse, but when society places less emphasis on covert forms of abuse, it increases the risk of people suffering in silence. Many survivors of non-physical forms of abuse may not even know that what's being done to them in their relationships is far from OK. Without awareness, some survivors may also unknowingly be perpetrators of abuse in some contexts, while simultaneously suffering abuse themselves. Read about the different forms of abuse on the diagram on the next page.

Which were the types of abuse you weren't previously aware of, if any?

Are there any other types of abuse you know of that aren't in the diagram?

Gaslighting

Let's look at gaslighting a little further, since it's arguably the most confusing form of abuse. Gaslighting can happen when someone:

*   Makes you doubt your own memory, e.g., insisting events never happened.
*   Tells you that you are crazy or have mental health concerns.
*   Tells you their abuse is "for your own good" (e.g., controlling your finances because they claim you're "so bad with money" / "like a child" with money).
*   Tells you are imagining or over-exaggerating their abusive behaviour.
*   Tells other people – including friends, the police, doctors, counsellors or legal professionals, etc. – that you are unstable, have mental health problems or substance abuse problems when you don't.
*   Tells you or others that *you* are the one being abusive towards them, when you're not or just defending yourself against their abuse / manipulative behaviours (sometimes referred to as 'victim-playing').

(Continue reading after diagram)

TYPES OF ABUSE

exploiting
Abuse, irrespective of its form(s), is all about power and control

1. GASLIGHTING
Manipulate (someone) using psychological methods into doubting their own sanity / interpretation of past events / memory / reasoning ability / logic.

2. PHYSICAL ABUSE
The most recognised form of abuse. Intentional bodily injury, incl. slapping, pinching, choking, kicking, shoving, inappropriately using drugs / physical restraints, refusing medical care and/or controlling medication, damaging personal property, coercion into substance abuse.

3. TECHNOLOGICAL ABUSE
Using technology to control / harass / stalk someone, e.g., hacking into email / personal accounts, using tracking devices in someone's cell phone to monitor their location, phone calls and messages, monitoring all interactions via social media, demanding to know someone's passwords and location at all times, sharing someone's intimate photos without consent (sometimes called revenge porn).

4. FINANCIAL ABUSE
Any behaviour that maintains power and control over finances, e.g., inflicting physical harm / injury that would prevent the person from attending work, harassing partner at their workplace, controlling financial assets and effectively putting the person on an allowance, damaging their credit score.

5. VISA ABUSE
Tactics of abuse that may be used against immigrant partners include destroying immigration papers, restricting partner from learning English, threatening to hurt partner's family in their home country, threatening to have partner deported.

6. SEXUAL ABUSE
Includes any sexual behaviours without a partner's consent, incl. forcing someone to have sex with other people (e.g., human trafficking), pursuing sexual activity when the victim is not fully conscious or is afraid to say no, hurting someone physically during sex, coercing someone to have sex without protection or sabotaging birth control.

7. EMOTIONAL / PSYCHOLOGICAL ABUSE
Controlling a person by, e.g., name calling / insulting, blaming them for all problems in the relationship, extreme jealousy, intimidation, shaming, humiliating, isolating them from their support network/others in general, controlling what a person does and where they go, stalking, embarrasses them in front of others, threatens self-harm/suicide so they do as asked.

**If you're currently experiencing family violence or abuse, please call 1800-RESPECT 1800-737-732 (Australia), or visit the global directories at https://nomoredirectory.org/ or https://www.hotpeachpages.net/a/countries.html if you are overseas

Sometimes, despite best efforts at gaining clarity on these situations, it can still feel very challenging to clearly tell if someone is being abusive or gaslighting you. A person who has been subjected to long-term, or a lifetime of gaslighting may have intense struggles with feeling like they could trust their own judgement on anything at all. However, if you ever asked yourself if you were being gaslit, it's possible that you already are.

NDs are often particularly vulnerable to gaslighting because we commonly experience a lifetime of challenges starting and/or keeping friendships and relationships. Being no stranger to self-doubt, many of us would go to great lengths to prove ourselves to someone and maintain relationships, leaving us especially unguarded against love-bombing from gaslighters (often involves showering us with over-the-top degree of attention, flattery and affection, to draw us into the trap of their manipulation later on).

Cycle of abuse

The cycle of abuse is a term coined by psychologist Lenore E. Walker after extensive observations and interviews with women who survived abuse and domestic violence. It's most frequently used in reference to physical abuse in intimate partner relationships, but it can really occur in any relationship (e.g., familial relationships/ friendships) and in any form of abuse (e.g., emotional abuse). 4 stages that tend to repeat in cycles in an abusive relationship were identified:

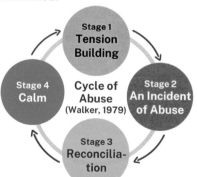

Please note: Even though this model serves as a useful reference in understanding abuse, it is not meant to be comprehensive of all abuse-related experiences. Additionally, the stages may not always happen in the same order, or in some case, calm and reconciliation may not happen at all.

Most people would be familiar with, or could guess, how Stages 1 and 2 would look like, but may not be aware of the roles that Stages 3 and 4 play in perpetuating this vicious cycle. So, let's have a look:

Stage 3: Reconciliation

After the incident of abuse, the abusive party may feel like the tension starts to dissipate, even though the abused party may have quite the opposite experience. Once that tension eases off, the abusive party may appear genuinely ashamed of their behaviours and motivated to make amends. They may apologise, shower you with affection, or promise they'll never do it again. They may seem romantic, supportive and loving. Because you care about them, you may be drawn to believe their words and give them another chance.

Stage 4: Calm

The abusive person may continue to be attentive but may start shifting from being apologetic to now excusing or minimising their abusive behaviours in ways, such as:

- Shifting responsibility, e.g., "If the waiter didn't do that, I wouldn't have got so angry and lost my temper with you."
- Justifying their abuse, e.g., "I'm sorry I [did X] but it was all because of [so-and-so]."
- Gaslighting you, e.g., "It really wasn't that big of a deal."

This stage can be confusing. Overt abusive behaviours may not have resurfaced, but there's now an underlying tone of dismissal or more covert forms of abuse that you may not immediately identify. In time, tension may start building again, and the cycle of abuse repeats.

Practice tuning in to your body cues

Anyone can say anything to us (e.g., "I love you", "I'm trying to help you", etc). Sadly, we can't *always* simply take what others tell us at surface value. When you wonder if someone's intentions and agenda actually match their words, try to notice the 'messages' that your body is trying to send you. When we actually feel loved, our bodies *don't* freeze up in response, for example. When we actually feel supported, our bodies don't generally feel like screaming or exploding or imploding in that moment. If you want to reflect on the messages that your body sends you in these situations, try the activity below (instructions are at the centre of the diagram). It's possible that this may be more helpful for some than others (e.g., if you have severe interoception struggles, this may feel challenging).

Examples: Throat tightens up   Sick in the stomach/ stomach 'flips'   Desire to inch away/ put distance

Feels need to plaster on a smile and maintain it

Holding breath

Mind goes blank/ mildly dissociate

"My dear, that's NOT love"
On these envelopes, write some ways that your body sends you a message that it may not actually be love (even when you're being told otherwise)

© Jasmine Loo Psychology 2023

Body shrinks to make self smaller   Body clamps up/ muscle tension   Jaw tightens/ clenching

Building Blocks of a Healthy Relationship

Consider this: there's no such thing as perfect or indestructible buildings. But what we use to build a house and how we build it can make a big difference to its resilience against natural elements. Which is why we don't build houses with random pieces of wood we find that may or may not be untreated, or build brick walls with the bricks stacked directly on top of each other, or build a house without laying a foundation.

Healthy relationships are kind of like a well-built house – they aren't invincible, but they tend to be sturdier and more resilient to harsh weather elements and pests. Similarly, being in healthy relationships doesn't mean that there'll never be any problems, and that we'd live happily ever after. *It's real life after all.* It can, however, mean a stronger foundation in the relationship, built from both parties' efforts, that helps overcome challenges that arise in an adaptive manner. Write some key building blocks you've identified below:

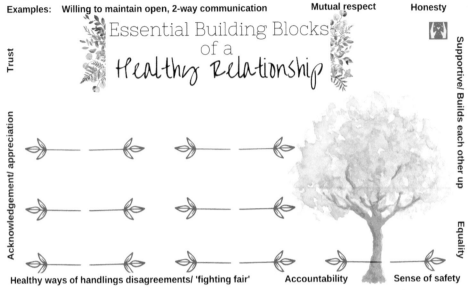

Examples: Willing to maintain open, 2-way communication   Mutual respect   Honesty

Trust

Supportive/ Builds each other up

Acknowledgement/ appreciation

Equality

Healthy ways of handlings disagreements/ 'fighting fair'   Accountability   Sense of safety

Several key building blocks specifically are worthy of further discussion:

1.   *Emotional accountability*

IMAGINE THIS SCENARIO:

You're walking your puppy at the park one fine day. Your puppy's walking calmly and he's just done his business. Let's just say picking up poop isn't your favourite thing to do, but you just got it over with.

All of a sudden, another puppy came darting towards yours, and the 2 hit it off immediately and played together SUPER excitedly. It was very cute and all, until the over-excitement got your puppy to go for a number 2 again...

And you look at the other puppy's owner and try to communicate with a knowing smile, "Well, this is really your poop to pick up. Your puppy got mine all excited. I'm not doing it again..." But they just look at you, thinking, "What...?" So, here's the question...   **"Whose poop is it?"**

In a sense, being human is a bit like owning a dog. Owning a dog means that you'll have poop to pick up on a regular basis. Being human means that you'll have emotions/feelings on a regular basis. What event correlates with, or causes, when or where your dog poops doesn't change the fact that you're still the one responsible for picking it up. Similarly, what event correlates with, or causes what emotions or feelings you experience doesn't change the fact that you're still the one responsible for your own feelings.

Conversely, others' feelings aren't our responsibility, no matter how much we care for them. We may care about and try to be gentle with their feelings, but none of us can be responsible for anyone else's feelings but our own. This is exactly what emotional accountability means. Our emotional experience may have to do with another person's actions, but that is only a part of the equation. Another important element is our unique perception of the event, or that person's actions, and with it, our reaction to them.

Having an emotional reaction to things is an inevitable part of being human, but it doesn't make it the other person's problem to solve. Emotional accountability from both parties makes space for finding constructive ways to communicate feelings with each other, and improves chances of finding a mutually workable solution (Chap. 6 discusses healthy communication).

Many late-identified NDs especially struggle with separating other people's emotions from their own (we'll be discussing this in detail in Chap. 7, when we look into alexithymia). Without support from early years support and being specifically introduced to the concept of emotional accountability, many may not be aware of it, let alone its importance in building healthy relationships.

Before this, was emotional accountability a concept that you were already familiar with? Is it something that you deem to be present in your key relationships currently?

_____

_____

_____

2.   *Retaining individuality*

Neither party in a healthy relationship should have to compromise who they are as a person – their individual identity. Each party should be comfortable continuing to spend time with, and to develop, their other relationships, as well as doing the things they love and enjoy. They'd be supportive of each other in pursuing new hobbies or make new relationships.

Seeing the other party as an extension of yourself (or the other way round) risks creating an unhealthy, enmeshed or co-dependent relationship, which can breed feelings of resentment and bitterness. An example may be parents who genuinely treat their children as their 'mini-me', who can achieve their unfulfilled dreams. We'll touch on this some more in the next chapter.

3.   *Acknowledge your unique relationship contributions*

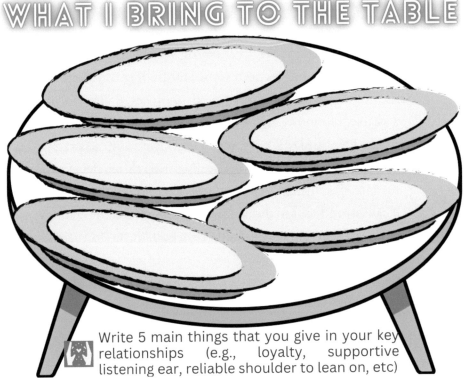

WHAT I BRING TO THE TABLE

Write 5 main things that you give in your key relationships (e.g., loyalty, supportive listening ear, reliable shoulder to lean on, etc)

Acknowledging and appreciating what you bring to the table in your valued relationships is important. As late-diagnosed/identified NDs, some of you may be used to thinking that there's nothing much of value that you could offer. Some of you may have the sorrow from harsh rejections in the past, but consider this scenario: Picture your loved one making a meal for you with all their heart. You take a look at the dishes on the table. Would you think, "Nothing has caviar in it, or is embellished with gold flakes, and oh, that looks a bit charred. Thanks, but no thanks"? No? Why not?

Because when someone you care about gives you the best that they have to offer, in the best way they know how to, it is meaningful. You don't care about the best ingredient there is out there in the world being made into the most exquisite delicacy. This is not to say no one in the world would think this way, but that if your loved one thought that way, then let's just say that what you bring to the relationship isn't likely the main issue there.

A chef who understands, appreciates and respects the ingredients they work with create dishes that reflect that. So, try to think and write some key things that you bring to your relationships on the plates in the pg. 68 diagram. If you really struggle, try asking one of your loved ones!

4.   *Insight on your own relationship needs*

Much of healthy relationships rests on healthy communication. The other party can never 'just know' our needs from the relationship if we don't openly communicate about them. But we can't possibly communicate what we don't know. Using the diagram on the next page, reflect on and fill out your key relationship needs. The neon-coloured circles can be the main relationship categories in your life (e.g., friendship, romantic relationship, family, etc), or specific key people in your life. Do whatever suits you! If you'd like an example, you can find one when you scan the QR code at the front of this book.

Depending on the nature of the relationship, the types of needs that are relevant may be different (e.g., sexual, communication of expectations, or social needs, etc). Don't be surprised or disheartened if you find this challenging to start, or find the full-page sized diagram a bit daunting. It's normal to struggle with something new but we can try anyway. As late-identified NDs, you might be used to spending a lot more time thinking about others' expectations (and if you're meeting them) than your own needs. So, the diagram is intentionally sized this way, so you can prioritise thinking about your needs.

My Key Relation-ship Needs

Emotion-al Needs

Emotion-al Needs

5.

BOUNDARIES & SELF-CARE FOR NEURODIVERGENTS

In this chapter, we'll be covering neurodivergent relational boundaries and self-care. If you're wondering why we merged these two topics, it's for no other reason than that it's almost impossible to truly care for ourselves without also maintaining healthy boundaries in our relationships. But first, a quick review. In the last chapter, we looked at:

- ◆ Healthy and unhealthy power dynamics in relationships, and the common red flags of an unhealthy or toxic relationship.
- ◆ Different types of abuse, as well as the cycle of abuse.
- ◆ Some fundamental building blocks to healthy relationships.

Fun fact: Do you know that in the Chinese languages (e.g., Mandarin, Cantonese, etc.), there isn't *exactly* a word for "boundaries" used in the context of relationships? There's a word for boundaries between countries, and to mean within the boundaries of laws and rules. A word for "bottom line" in the interpersonal context (so that things may seem completely fine until you've crossed someone's bottom line, then it's *really* not fine). But none for relational boundaries. Not traditionally, anyway. Hopefully by now, there'd be decent awareness, and a word has been specifically created for it.

Many people (of varying neurotypes) may misunderstand having

71

boundaries as being synonymous to 'keeping everyone at arm's length', which implies the inability to form close relationships or the lack of desire for closeness with others. This could not be further from the truth. In fact, maintaining healthy boundaries in any relationships – close or distant – is crucial for maintaining the health of our cherished relationships.

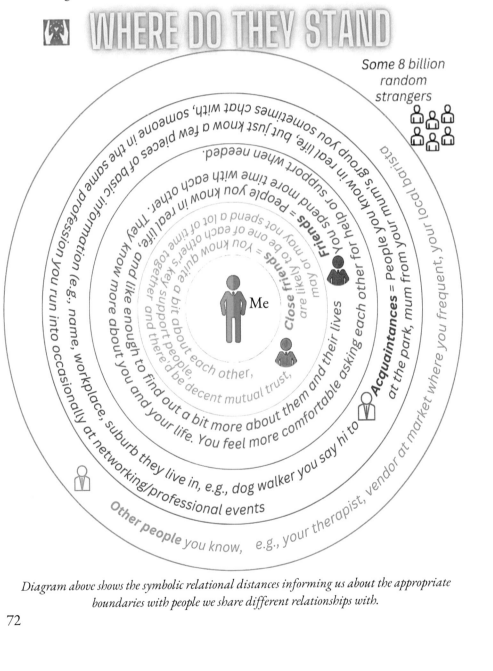

Diagram above shows the symbolic relational distances informing us about the appropriate boundaries with people we share different relationships with.

Late-Identification of Neurodivergence and Healthy Boundaries – What's the Connection?

Since 'people pleasing' tends to be a common struggle for many NDs, establishing and maintaining healthy boundaries in relationships can be tricky. The capacity for establishing healthy boundaries is tied closely to a person's self-identity because, just like boundaries between countries, how do we define boundaries if we aren't certain where one ends, and where the rest of the world starts? If we have not yet formed clear ideas of who we are, what's ours and what's not? The fact that you've flown under the radar for so long suggests that there's probably been heavy masking involved.

Sadly, since everyone has a finite amount of time and resources, and so much of NDs' time and energy is often put into learning to mask as a survival mechanism in a neurotypical world, there may not be much left for the self-discovery necessary to form a solid self-identity. For many late-identified NDs, unfortunately their boundaries have also likely been repeatedly crossed throughout their lives. The pressure to conform to NT ways of *being* that may feel extremely uncomfortable for them (e.g., maintaining eye contact, sitting still), to endure the pain from being flooded with sensory hypersensitivities for long periods of time (e.g., the noise at school every day), to suppress healthy stimming behaviours – just to name a few. Sound all too familiar?

Having said that, do you see what this means? It means you've done many more difficult things than you gave yourself credit for. Did you choose that? No. Does it justify the hardship you were put through? No. But what I'm saying is... *You've done so many difficult things in life. You. You have.* So, yes, learning to build healthy boundaries and to care for yourself is a challenging, lifelong learning process. In fact, none of the things covered in this book are easy to practice in real life.

But you've done all these challenging things in life that you didn't even choose to for the sake of others' convenience and comfort. You can do challenging things that contribute to your own wellbeing, too. You deserve to reap the benefits of your own hard work, too. So... Shall we get started?

Look at the diagram below that explains boundaries in close relationships. You can think of it this way: Pretend each of us has a hula hoop around us. When we first get to know someone, the size of the hula hoops is usually huge. In time, if we get to know each other more, earn each other's trust and grow closer, we gradually trade the hula hoops to smaller sizes. However, the bottom line in a healthy relationship is that, regardless of closeness, there should always be 2 individual hula hoops. Neither party should try to barge into another's hula hoop by overlapping them.

Boundaries in Close Relationships
© Jasmine Loo Psychology 2023

Healthy
- Free to be their own persons
- Communicate and negotiate different needs with each other, but doesn't impose/ control
- Relationship has "breathing space for both"

Unhealthy
- Lacks individuality
- One/both parties often perceive they "have the right" to tell the other what to think/ feel/ decide
- Attempts to maintain/develop self-identity from either/both parties may create friction in relationship at times

Enmeshed Relationship
- One/both parties lose their respective identities outside of who they are in the relationship
- Any attempts to express own thoughts/needs may be seen as a betrayal to the other party
- Creates a "suffocating" feeling for either/both

✳**Lacking Boundaries ≠ Closeness/Intimacy**

How does it compare to how healthy boundaries look if the relationship isn't all that close, then?

Something like this, for example

*In general, are healthy boundaries something that you find easy or difficult to navigate? Why do you think that's the case?*_____

_____

_____

_____

_____

Are there particular relationships/contexts that you find harder to establish or maintain healthy boundaries in compared to others? If so, why is that? _____

_____

_____

_____

_____

_____

_____

Common Pitfall that Can Lead to Unhealthy Boundaries

It's not uncommon for people struggling with forming healthy boundaries to express their desire to help or to be polite. It's important to clarify that being altruistic and wanting to be kind and helpful to others is a wonderful thing and *isn't* an issue. It's when we go down that slippery slope of shifting our boundaries a tiny bit at a time until we eventually cross the line of being a 'martyr' (i.e., self-sacrificing for others) that it becomes an issue. It's tricky because as with any kinds of slippery slopes, it usually starts with very reasonable and acceptable shifts in boundaries, and each shift may be so small that we aren't generally alarmed about it.

Healthy boundaries have an appropriate degree of flexibility to it. For example, you may not usually consider offering to take care of all the housework for the apartment you share with your good friend, but they broke their arm, which is now in a cast. After weighing up your options, you decide that it's still manageable for you in the short-term and offer to do all the chores around the house until your housemate's cast is off. It may mean temporarily sacrificing some rest and social time, but you're willing to help. Having some flexibility in our boundaries help keep it healthy - to this point.

You might start going down a slippery slope when, for instance, after your friend's cast is off, they ask for your help for another week because they have so many errands to catch up on. You might feel hesitant, but you tell yourself,

"What's another week?" and agree to it. Suppose that after the week, they tell you that they've been really stressed out from life commitments and asked for your continued support with chores while they get sorted...

In such situations, if we continue to push our own boundaries, eventually we might feel bitter and resentful towards our housemate and the relationship. If we have multiple of these situations or relationships occurring concurrently, we're most probably headed for burnout.

Understanding how healthy and unhealthy boundaries look like in different relationships is an essential foundation to lay before we can reflect on where our boundaries lie, and learn ways to communicate and maintain our boundaries with others (which we'll be covering in the next chapter!).

For now, let's move onto topic of self-care and why it's such an important life skill to practice for late-identified NDs. To many, "self-care" may be perceived as an intrinsic ability, but for many NDs, true neurodivergent-style self-care may be a learned skill after all the years of masking. It's therefore unsurprising that ND burnout is so common.

Autistic/ADHD Burnout

Challenges with relational boundaries, constant monitoring and analysing 'appropriateness' of behaviour or performance, sensory dysregulation, struggling to fit in, perfectionism, executive dysfunction – these are just some common things constantly running in the background for NDs, just like phone background apps that silently drain its battery.

Except, NDs don't really have an option to simply turn these background apps off (but we can certainly try to manage some degree of these – stay tuned!). This hasn't even taken into account some possible 'background apps' that might differ from ND to ND (e.g., complex trauma, life stressors, mental health struggles, sleep and health issues, etc). This is all BEFORE the day's many demands even start coming at us. *Still wonder why you're constantly so tired?*

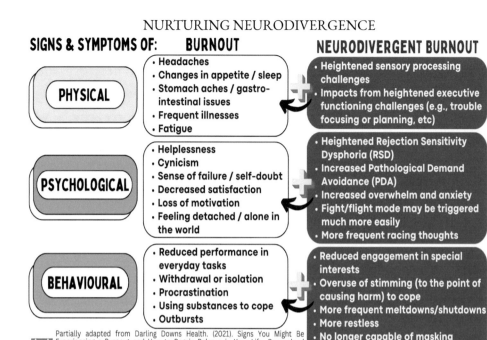

SIGNS & SYMPTOMS OF: BURNOUT — NEURODIVERGENT BURNOUT

PHYSICAL
- Headaches
- Changes in appetite / sleep
- Stomach aches / gastro-intestinal issues
- Frequent illnesses
- Fatigue

+
- Heightened sensory processing challenges
- Impacts from heightened executive functioning challenges (e.g., trouble focusing or planning, etc)

PSYCHOLOGICAL
- Helplessness
- Cynicism
- Sense of failure / self-doubt
- Decreased satisfaction
- Loss of motivation
- Feeling detached / alone in the world

+
- Heightened Rejection Sensitivity Dysphoria (RSD)
- Increased Pathological Demand Avoidance (PDA)
- Increased overwhelm and anxiety
- Fight/flight mode may be triggered much more easily
- More frequent racing thoughts

BEHAVIOURAL
- Reduced performance in everyday tasks
- Withdrawal or isolation
- Procrastination
- Using substances to cope
- Outbursts

+
- Reduced engagement in special interests
- Overuse of stimming (to the point of causing harm) to cope
- More frequent meltdowns/shutdowns
- More restless
- No longer capable of masking
- Significant neglect of basic self-care (e.g., showering, etc)

Partially adapted from Darling Downs Health. (2021). Signs You Might Be Experiencing a Burnout and How to Regain Balance in Your Life. Queensland Government. Retrieved from https://www.darlingdowns.health.qld.gov.au/about-us/our-stories/feature-articles/signs-you-might-be-experiencing-a-burnout-and-how-to-regain-balance-in-your-life

As we previously discussed, masking is often something that most late-identified NDs are familiar with. Have you ever reflected on the types of masking behaviours you find most draining? Write them in the clouds below!

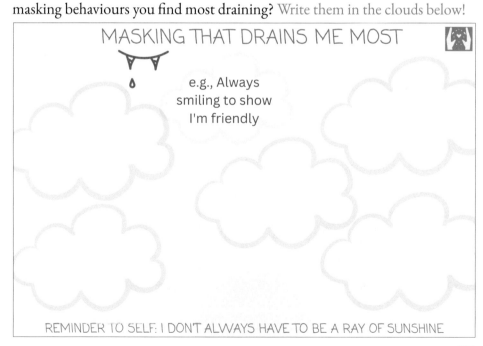

MASKING THAT DRAINS ME MOST

e.g., Always smiling to show I'm friendly

REMINDER TO SELF: I DON'T ALWAYS HAVE TO BE A RAY OF SUNSHINE

That said, just because we don't necessarily have control over the amount of background apps we have running, or perhaps the needed necessary 'apps' (i.e., particular commitments, events and activities in a day) on particular days or periods of our lives, it doesn't mean that we cannot also carry extra 'power banks' with us to avoid running out of charge. Think of 'power banks' as activities or behaviours we can engage in to make up for the power that gets drained by the commitments through the day.

'Power banks' could be a period of time (e.g., 15-min, an hour, etc) carved out for solitary time or for engaging in special interests, or an evening relaxing with minimal sensory stimulation (e.g., dark and quiet space). They could also be a regular block of time reserved for engaging in healthy stimming (check out the Stim Menus at the end of chapter for ideas), or daily opportunities to be around our safe person to buffer against 'draining apps'. Use the chart on the next page in either of the ways below to help you practice planning ahead, or doing daily retrospective reflections in order to help prevent burnout:

Method 1: Try plotting out some of the things that drained you today in the red column, and some other things that you have done throughout the day, or can do for the rest of the day to recharge before the day ends.

Method 2: Try thinking about what you expect tomorrow to look like in the same manner, so that you can anticipate whether it would help to incorporate more 'power banks' in the next day as a pre-emptive measure.

Think of how much something would drain or recharge your energy levels by allocating a percentage to each of them - from 1% for something that drains or recharges you the slightest to 100% for something that drains or recharges you fully. Add up the numbers in each column to get a total number for each. Then, find out whether you're 'in the red' by subtracting Total A from Total B. Remember, just because your Grand Total has been in the green zone, it doesn't always mean you won't enter burnout (remember there are still background apps to account for!). However, if you've consistently been in the red zone, then it's probably safe to say that you'd most probably experience burnout at some point.

Battery Health
DAILY REPORT

DATE:

'BATTERY USAGE'		'POWER BANKS'	
EVENT/ ACTIVITY	DRAINAGE (0-100%)	EVENT/ ACTIVITY	CHARGING (0-100%)

Total (A):   Total (B):

Grand Total (Total B - Total A):

If the grand total is "in the red"/a negative number, what can I do tomorrow to 'turbo-charge'?

*Remember to refer to my Self-Care Menu for ideas to incorporate more recharging "power banks" into my day.

It should also be noted that every ND presents differently when they're drained and low in capacity. For one person, they may have no issues responding verbally to others, but may struggle to respond with any tone of voice or facial expressions. For another, they might struggle with vocalising.

When our phones are running out of charge, we usually set it to 'Power Saving Mode' (or equivalent, depending on the type of phone you have) to preserve the battery charge, in hopes that it'll last us to the end of the day, when we're able to recharge it. In Power Saving mode, the screen's brightness may be reduced, Bluetooth may be turned off and some non-essential apps may be turned off. If that's still insufficient, we may later put the phone into Ultra Power Saving mode, which might shut off all non-essential apps and Wi-Fi. Only the bare essential functions remain.

Being neurodivergent is not so different here. The dynamic nature of neurodivergence means that our level of capacity from day to day, moment to moment may differ, depending on factors, such as our sleep quality the night before, if we're sick, if we've been under stress or are feeling very emotional. At times, our capacities might drop quickly and unexpectedly, and we may enter (or may even be involuntarily forced into) an ND-version of Power Saving mode or Ultra Power Saving mode, leaving only the bare essential functions.

However, for many NDs, the closest, key support people may or may not be aware of the cues that suggest that their beloved ND has entered one of these modes, and may unintentionally do things that are unhelpful in those situations. Or, they might be able to tell that support is needed but may not know what's helpful for the person.

Use the cue cards on the next page to help your trusted support people know the main cues to be aware of that tells them you're in either of these modes. Try to make the points clear and concise. Think of the things that are observable for another person who cannot read your mind (what would they *see* or *hear*, or, what are the things that they might stop seeing and hearing, but usually would?). Then, use the cue cards beneath them to specify the top 3 helpful and unhelpful things others can do when you're in any of these modes.

These cue cards are a practical tool to help you clearly communicate your support needs in this regard with your support person(s) in advance because when we're in either of these modes, we generally don't have the capacity to engage in this sort of communication (Scan QR code on the Copyrights page at the front of the book to download and print out the full-sized cards).

Then, use the Self-Care Menu on the next page to help you plot out some 'power bank' options. When we're tired, the last thing we'd like to do, or are capable of doing, is to plan or think of what to do for self-care. So, if you're thinking, "I already know what I'd do, I don't need to write it down," *resist the temptation*. Have the menu at an easily accessible location, so that when you need it, all you need to do is to pick something from your menu.

Reminder: Self-care doesn't necessarily have to be fancy, Insta-worthy, time-consuming or expensive. Sure, when we can afford the time and money, no harm treating ourselves to a spa day for self-care or cook a fancy meal, if that's what we enjoy. But self-care can be a simpler, everyday activity that recharges us, e.g., going to bed on time to catch up on sleep, or turning off work emails and social media every evening.

MY SELF-CARE MENU

DOs:
(INCLUDE/ DO MORE OF)

DON'Ts:
(STOP DOING/ DO LESS OF)

REGULAR DAY-TO-DAY SELF-CARE

1

2

3

4

5

6

1

2

3

4

5

6

TURBO MODE SELF-CARE
FOR THE TOUGH DAYS

7

8

9

7

8

9

Healthy Stims as Part of Your Self-Care Menu

You'd have seen the term "healthy stims" pop up here and there in this book, and may wonder what it meant. For the longest time, neurodivergent special interests and stims (i.e., repetitive behaviours) have often been treated as something weird or strange, something that draws negative attention from others, something to be suppressed. Stims are generally NDs' ways of experiencing the world, of regulating or expressing ourselves and our emotions. They aren't what most NTs are used to seeing, but most of them aren't a problem at all, and can instead be very beneficial for NDs. Masking and suppressing stims, on the other hand, can be harmful for NDs.

Nevertheless, it's probably fair to say that as NDs, moderation isn't exactly our forte. And we can definitely have too much of even a good thing. Some individuals stim so frequently and intensely that they can end up with bone malformation or other painful results. Having the space to stim for an ND is like having the space to breathe – it's helpful when NDs can flexibly engage in and disengage from the stims. If you struggle to disengage from stimming in general or from particular stims, even when it starts to hurt you, consider reflecting on the sustainability of your current lifestyle. If it's not sustainable, can you, or your support network can do anything to reduce life demands while you recover? Can any changes in your environment be made to minimise the drain on you? No amount of power banks can help in the long run, if something continuously drains significant amounts of charge.

Another possible scenario where stimming can be harmful or even dangerous is where it involves any self-harming or self-injurious behaviours. Head-banging is a commonly known one, but others, such as skin picking, hair pulling, and repeatedly punching or pinching yourself also fall under this category. In fact, some of these can develop into clinical concerns, such as excoriation disorder (also skin-picking disorder, or dermatillomania) and trichotillomania (also hair-pulling disorder), if left unaddressed.

Now that we've gone through situations where stimming can potentially be problematic, let's circle back to healthy stimming. Have you ever reflected on your sensory profile (c.f. mind maps on Chapters 1 and 2), and thought about healthy stims that you might enjoy and fit your sensory profile?

Check out the Stim Menus below for ideas to make up your own!

Stimming ideas for visual sensory-seekers.

Stimming ideas for tactile sensory-seekers.

Auditory Menu

Ideas for Stims

Remember that these are all just ideas. Not everything will work for everyone - find out what works for you and develop your own menu!

PINK NOISE / NATURE SOUNDS

Examples include: waves lapping on the beach, leaves rustling in the trees, or a steady rainfall.

STEPPING ON CRUNCHY LEAVES

Go out of your way to step on some crunchy leaves in the colder months. Listen to the sounds.

MUSIC THAT FUELS YOUR SOUL

Have playlists for every mood/ state that you can play on repeat, e.g.,

- A 'wake up' playlist
- A 'winding down' playlist
- A "hopeful, upbeat' playlist when working through that to-do list
- An 'angry at the world' playlist to defuse some of that energy on select days

Vocal Stims Menu

HUMMING

WHISTLING

ADD-A-TUNE-TO-IT

Random phrase stuck in your head on repeat all day? Why not add a fun tune and a sick beat to it?

Stimming ideas for those who are sensory-seeking with sounds.

VESTIBULAR MENU
Stim Ideas

*Discontinue immediately if you experience any discomfort or motion sickness when trying these ideas. Always consult your medical practitioner beforehand to ensure suitability of use. Remember to check the maximum weight capacity of each product before purchasing.

SENSORY SWINGS

ADULT TRAMPOLINE

HAMMOCK CHAIRS

WOBBLE STOOL FOR ADULTS

ROLLER COASTERS
Why not?

STEPPING STONE MATS

ROCKING CHAIRS

YOGA BALLS

JLP does not have any affiliations with companies selling these products nor endorse any products. Product links are for reference only and are not affiliated with JLP.

Stimming ideas for vestibular sensory-seekers (may manifest as hyperactivity).

Proprioception Menu
[pro·pree·oh·sep·shn]

IDEAS FOR STIMS & SELF-CARE ACTIVITIES

Always consult a medical practitioner before trying out any of these ideas to ensure suitability. Discontinue immediately if you experience any discomfort or pain. Remember to check the weight recommendations for products and follow professional and personalised guidance from qualified trainers for exercise and heavy work routines.

WEIGHTED BLANKETS

THERAPY PUTTY

DEEP PRESSURE MASSAGES

SWIMMING

TIGHT HUGS

BODY SOCK/ COMPRESSION SHEETS

GARDENING

MUSCULAR ENDURANCE WORKOUTS

YOGA

CHEWY NECKLACE

KNEADING DOUGH (FOR BAKING)

CHEWING GUM

Stimming ideas for proprioceptive sensory seekers.

Olfactory Menu
Ideas for Stims / Self-Care Activities

Remember that these are all just ideas. Not everything is right for everyone - find out what works for you and develop your own menu! Always consult your GP beforehand if unsure of allergies. Never leave candles unattended as it could be a fire risk.

Plant a herb garden to make herb pouches you can carry with you

Essential oils with smells you like

Smell of fresh bread (homemade/bakery)

Spend time to take in the scent of your morning coffee with each sip

Open windows/ have nature walks after the rain for the 'smell of rain'

Spend time in bookshops for the smell of new books

Dried flower pouches (e.g., rose, lavender, etc)

Perfumes/ Cologne

Scented candles

Smell of the ocean by the seaside

Stimming ideas for those who are sensory-seeking with smells.

6.

HEALTHY COMMUNICATION STRATEGIES FOR NEURODIVERGENTS

Hopefully last chapter has given you some ideas on self-care, and that you've had a chance to engage in some self-care. A quick review of what we covered last chapter:

- Relational boundaries, and healthy and unhealthy boundaries.
- Discussed the risks of ND burnout, and the role that poor relational boundaries can play in ND burnout.
- Provided some practical tools to help you plan for self-care.
- Gave you some ideas on healthy stimming with Stim Menus.

This chapter, we'll be looking at healthy communication strategies for NDs, which are one of the most important tools to help build healthy relationships.

Let's Take a Dip into NT Social Communication Strategies

Truth is, when you're talking to someone and it *just works*, I wouldn't really bother with strategies at all. You might remember that I'm a big believer of 'do what works'. However, from time to time, many NDs might find themselves in situations where they'd very much like to engage in a conversation with someone, but wouldn't mind if they could just reach into their bag and pull out a strategy to help keep the conversation flowing, so to speak. In that case, you might find the visual below helpful:

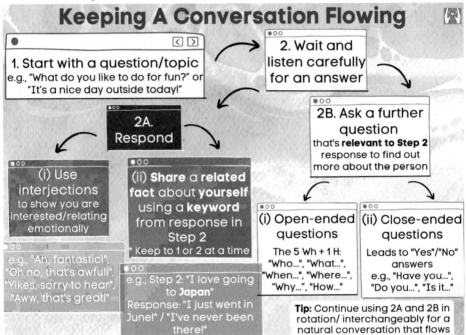

When we see the term "social skills training", what it generally means is "learn ways to behave like a NT in social settings". In other words, learn to mask your ND traits. As discussed in Chap. 3, excessive masking can be harmful. At the same time, we also live in a far-from-ideal world, where NTs, as its name suggests, make up the majority of society. One way to look at learning NT communication strategies is that it's not vastly different from learning English as a second language as someone born and raised in Asia, like myself.

The English language is a widely used language across the world (yes, it's largely due to colonisation, but still) - we learn it because we want the possible ease of communicating with as many other people around the world as possible for a variety of reasons. While in theory, we shouldn't have to learn English to live in a country like Australia, for example, there might be some practical benefits to having some English proficiency and a willingness to use it when it suits your needs, and when you deem the cost of using it is bearable.

Nevertheless, there may be times when a bilingual English speaker may choose not to speak English at all for a range of reasons. For instance, when they're conversing with a non-English speaking person who speaks one of the other languages they speak. Or when they don't want to appear like a tourist in the countries where they speak the language. Bottom line is, a bilingual speaker has a choice of when to exercise that knowledge as they go along.

'Speaking NT' can be perceived as analogous to learning an additional 'language' as a part of our personal toolkit to help us navigate life. Irrespective of whether your proficiency level is 'expert' or 'foundational', the most important thing is that you aren't seeing it, or being made to see it as your only language option, and that you can exercise your autonomy of when to use it, if at all.

Being pressured to live like a NT, on the other hand, is like forced cultural assimilation in the ethnocultural context, which is condemned in modern society. Hence, NDs who may not speak NT at all for any reasons (by choice or not) need to be treated with respect from society. *Are there any NT communication strategies that you'd like to further develop? If so, what are they, and why?*

_____

_____

Do you have any favourite ND communication styles (e.g., info-dumping, 'parallel play')? If so, describe them here. _____

_____

_____

Healthy and Unhealthy Communication Styles

There are 4 main styles of communication: aggressive, passive, passive aggressive and assertive. Of the four, assertive communication is generally the healthiest form of communication, even though context is still extremely important. For instance, it's probably a bad idea to be assertive when someone armed is mugging us because doing so might put us in harm's way.

Passiveness as a main mode of communication generally means that we're constantly putting our needs and feelings beneath everyone else's. If aggressiveness is like a red, hot blaze that burns through relationships, then passive-aggressiveness is akin to a slow poison. It's used when we're really trying to inflict some form of pain or damage to the other party, but at the same time hoping we won't have to pay the price for being directly aggressive (e.g., others' retaliation, damage to our 'image', criminal charges, etc). And we're not talking about ND witty sarcasm or dark humour here, no. Those are exempted (not clinically proven, but still).

An example of passive-aggressiveness may be when we're upset by someone else's actions, but instead of communicating our feelings assertively, we say, "Oh, that's no biggie at all, no one cares how I feel anyway". It could even come across as psychological manipulation in some contexts. For instance, instead of assertively asking for support from our children, we say something like, "You never visit me. If I were to slip in the shower one day, no one will even realise for days". While no one gets punched in the face, you can imagine why it can still do substantial harm to the health of a relationship.

What does assertive communication involve, exactly?

Previously, we reflected on our own relational needs and discussed healthy boundaries. It all sounded great, but you may have been asking, "*How?*". How do we communicate our relationship needs and establish boundaries with other people? Assertive communication is the medium that helps us get these important ideas through to another person to help build healthy relationships. Being assertive doesn't necessarily mean that others will then do exactly what we want, how we want it – that's coercive or overt control. Others' behaviours, choices thoughts and feelings are never within our circle of control.

Being assertive means that we have the tools to ask for what we want, and to decline requests that don't fit with what we want. The tools to share with someone our needs and perspectives, thoughts and feelings, without imposing them on the person. Two main components to assertive communication are: (1) the message is clear and direct (e.g., "I'd appreciate if you can take out the trash tonight, please" versus "I wish I didn't have to take out the trash"), and (2) calm and respectful manner in the delivery of message. *Of the 4 communication styles, which style would you say is your default?*_____

*Is there someone or something in your life that you attribute to being a major influence in the way you approach communication so far? How so?*_____

_____

_____

_____

_____

_____

_____

Reports of struggles with assertiveness amongst late-identified NDs are relatively common. This may have to do with a lifetime of being told off for being too direct (e.g., shamed for 'having no filter') and being expected to mask (e.g., being told to smile, be polite and keep quiet if you're uncomfortable about something said). Some NDs may have been in unhealthy or abusive relationships that conditioned them to believe that their voice, needs and wants are insignificant. Some may even feel unsafe using their voice. Understand that when we try to transform some of our deeply-rooted patterns of behaviour, it's a process that can take time and patience. *Growing up, was there anyone to teach you/ model what assertive communication looks like? How did that affect your assertiveness presently?*_____

_____

_____

_____

_____

_____

*How does your body feel when you consider asserting your needs/rights?*_____

_____

_____

_____

6. ND HEALTHY COMMUNICATION

SCRIPTS FOR CLEARLY SAYING NO

MOST DIRECT

1. NO.
2. I'M NOT INTERESTED.
3. THANKS, BUT NO THANKS.
4. I'M AFRAID I CAN'T DO THAT.
5. UNFORTUNATELY, I DON'T HAVE THE BANDWITH FOR THAT NOW.
6. I WISH I COULD, BUT NO.
7. I'M HONOURED/FLATTERED, BUT I CAN'T.
8. I APPRECIATE THE OFFER, BUT I'M BUSY.
9. THANK YOU FOR ASKING! I'D BE INTERESTED IN HEARING MORE, BUT I CAN'T THIS MONTH.
10. SORRY, I HAVE A LOT OF MY PLATE NOW, BUT MAYBE SOME OTHER TIME?

LEAST DIRECT

Understand and remember that... "Others have the right to request, and I have the right to accept or decline".

What are some underlying assumptions/beliefs you currently hold about your rights that affects your engagement in assertive communication with others around you (e.g., "others' needs are more important than mine")? _____

_____

_____

_____

_____

So, don't beat yourself up if this isn't something you feel ready to start practising right now. Practising being kind to yourself helps build a healthier self-view, which then helps you practice perceiving your needs and perspectives and feelings to be equally important as others' (remember the see-saw from Chap. 4?). This can then help you gain the confidence and motivation to practice assertiveness, starting from relationships you feel safe in. When you feel ready, you can try the strategies in the following sections.

Language use in assertive communication

Most of us know that the way a message is phrased can make a big difference in how it's received by others, whether it's in the context of asserting our feelings and needs, or resolving conflicts. The health and closeness of a relationship isn't necessarily determined by the lack of disagreements and even conflicts, but in *how* we *handle* differences, disagreements and conflicts. Many NDs find the strategies below helpful with assertive communication, be it written or verbal:

1.   ***Making "I-statements".***

I-statements help convey a sense of emotional accountability (c.f. Chap. 4), instead of blame from You-statements, which can help reduce defensiveness in the listener. What's better, there is an I-statement 'formula' that we can follow, which is laid out on the next page:

"I feel [emotion] when [event] happens. I'd appreciate if in the future we/you can please [insert your proposed solution]."

Let's compare an example of I-statement versus You-statement.

I-statement: *"I feel frustrated when you struggle to take initiative to help me out with chores. I'd like it if you could proactively share chores without repeated reminders from now on."*

You-statement: *"You never help me out with chores unless I ask you to."*

How would you feel if someone used an I-statement with you? _____

_____

_____

_____

_____

How would you feel if you are on the receiving end of the You-statement above?

_____

_____

_____

_____

Of the two, do you have a preference as a listener? Why so? _____

_____

_____

(Continue on the next page)   93

Which of the 2 do you use more often as a speaker in your day-to-day? If you're unsure, try paying attention to the way you speak from here on. _____

_____

_____

2. *Avoid resorting to absolutes and personal attacks.*

Most of us would usually agree that verbally attacking someone is unacceptable because that's resorting to aggressiveness, but we're all human. When we feel very angry or hurt by something that someone did, in the heat of the moment, the temptation to spew out the most hurtful words we could find in the moment may be strong. Practising assertiveness also acts as a self-reminder to focus on specific behaviours or actions that we have an issue with (which promotes collaborative problem-solving), *not* the person as a whole (which can evoke defensiveness and shame, and hurt the relationship).

There may be times when we might realise that there are so many things in a relationship that we take issue with, it's as if we have issues with the person as a whole. If that's the case, depending on circumstances and context, perhaps keeping distance with the person would be a more sound solution than resorting to personal attacks. A cue on whether we may be bordering on, or are engaging in personal attacks in our communication is when we start using absolutes more frequently. Absolutes are words that indicate the extreme ends of that frequency that something happens, e.g., "always" or "never". Another cue to alert us is when we hear our own voices calling the other person names (e.g., "You're so *lazy*. You *never* do anything around the house").

If we ever hear ourselves name-calling and using absolutes, let that be a cue for us to practice 'hitting pause' on the exchange with the other person, before we become more and more worked up emotionally. We can either create a safe exit by suggesting to resume the discussion when we're more collected with our thoughts, or acknowledge that it was unfair for us to name-call, and sincerely apologise before starting again. Practising accountability in our own communication is part of being assertive, too.

3.   *The broken-record technique.*

Sometimes, we may find ourselves in a frustrating situation where we have to uphold our boundaries with someone who's very persistent (if for any reason, you're unable to simply put some distance between you or disengage from the exchange). For instance, you might have a customer at work who's insistent on getting free repairs outside of warranty. Or a boundary-pushing family member whom you have no plans of severing ties with.

The broken-record technique is as the name suggests – to repeat yourself for as many times as needed without any creativity or even much emotional variation (this technique is best delivered in a calm and neutral manner; refer to section below). If you think, "Oh, how boring!", well, that's *exactly the point*! Check out this example below:

> Them: *"If you speak with X, you'll see differently about this"*
> You: *"I hear you, but I cannot do that"*.
> Them: *"I don't deserve this treatment... [and so on...]"*
> You: *"I hear you, but I can't do that"*.
> Them: *"You're not listening, I'm telling you..."*
> You: *"Yes, and I explained that I cannot do so"*.

The non-verbal in assertive communication

70% of communication is in the non-verbal parts of communication, and some may confuse assertiveness as aggressiveness, or vice versa. Grasping the differences can help us: (1) tell if someone's being aggressive or assertive with us, thereby informing how we should respond, and (2) be mindful of whether we may be presenting as aggressive or assertive, and if that fits with how we'd like to present in that context. Even when the exact same words are spoken, our tone of voice, body language and facial expressions can make a massive difference.

Consider this example: A restaurant customer says to a waiter, "This (dish) is too salty for me". Saying it in a calm voice, with a relaxed facial expression, versus standing up, towering over the poor waiter with a menacing expression, and half-screaming the exact same sentence have very different implications. Read through the infographics below on the non-verbal communication differences between aggressiveness and assertiveness. Remember that these aren't exhaustive, and to always take context into account.

AGGRESSIVENESS

Facial expressions

- Stares or glares that last for a long time
- Snarls
- Redness of the face, lowered brow, showing teeth, scowling or sneering

Voice & language

- Raised volume of voice
- Intimidating tone of voice
- Saying hurtful things they may or may not mean

Body language & behaviours

- Space invading
- Inappropriate gestures that make someone feel uncomfortable/ unsafe
- Mock attacks, (e.g., shaking fists, head-butts, leg-swinging)
- Touching without permission (e.g., grabbing someone's arm, prodding their chest)
- Breaking things / damaging items within the vicinity of the other person
- Dominating / threatening body posture
- Finger pointing

Assertiveness

Facial expressions

- Steady eye contact (for NTs/ NDs who don't struggle with eye contact)
- Calm & relaxed facial expression

Voice & language

- Confident voice (loud enough to be heard, but not raised)
- Calm but firm tone
- Respectful & clear language

Body language & behaviours

- Any movements are smooth and steady (vs sudden & unpredictable)
- Body upright, head up & shoulders relaxed
- Feet are firmly planted (i.e., flat on the floor & slightly apart to form a firm base, including when seated)
- Open body language (e.g., arms hang down, instead of crossed)
- Mindful & respectful of personal space
- Instead of finger pointing, indicate with an open palm with fingers together
- Listens & responds to others' concerns

*Is your current general style of communication aligned with the type of communicator you would like to be? Why or why not?*_____

_____

_____

_____

_____

_____

_____

_____

_____

How do you think your main communication style affects the health of your relationships? _____

_____

_____

_____

_____

Can you think of someone (real or fictional) who adopts a communication style that you wish to practice more going forward? Write a few specific things you admire about their communication style(s). _____

_____

_____

_____

_____

_____

_____

_____

_____

*Tip: If you wrote about someone you'd consider a role model above, try to see if you could, from time to time, take a moment to reflect on how you could draw inspiration from that person in your communication with others, e.g., try asking yourself questions, such as "How would X approach this with the other person?", or "What would X's demeanour be like?"

The price of assertiveness

My valued mentor used to say, "Life is a series of trade-offs", or something along those lines. We trade our time and effort for income, income for necessities, exposure to sponsored ads for use of free apps, partial freedom for protection of the law, etc. In other words, there's truly no free lunch in life, just different 'currencies' that we might pay in. Nothing can be all positives and no negatives. Being assertive is no different. We've discussed its benefits, but what might be the price for being assertive?

If we've been unassertive in our relationships and others have been used to, and perhaps also benefitted, from our lack of assertiveness, our new introduction of healthy boundaries and assertiveness would likely be met with resistance to varying degrees. We might even experience an escalation of boundary-crossing behaviours that consciously or unconsciously serve as an attempt to restore the old dynamics of the relationship (i.e., so that the other person can continue to benefit from our unassertiveness).

Starting to practice assertiveness can be painful, especially if unbalanced power dynamics have been the norm for most of our close relationships. It's not going to be easy because it'll most likely involve more than solely perfecting the skill. Therefore, this is a choice that only you, and you alone, can make. Remember that this doesn't have to be all-or-nothing – it's ***not true*** that you can only either be an assertive or unassertive person.

If you choose to start practising assertiveness, it only means that you're starting to slowly build upon times in your life when you're being assertive, to a degree you decide is right for you (i.e., the frequency in which you practise it in your day-to-day, or the specific relationships or contexts that you'd like to exercise it more than the others).

Many people choose to start practising assertiveness in relationships they already feel safe in before generalising it to more and more of other situations in their lives as they get more confident. Anyway, when it comes to tough decision-making, I *love* a good ole' cost-benefit breakdown to help lay out all that both options have to offer me (example template on the next page):

Cost-Benefit Analysis

Problem Statement: To be or not to be (assertive)

① **Practising Assertiveness**

Possible Costs	Possible Benefits

Current significance to me	Current significance to me

② **Not Practising Assertiveness**

Possible Costs	Possible Benefits

Current significance to me	Current significance to me

My current preference / choice:

Listening Skills for NDs

Knowing what to say, and how to say it, is just one-half of healthy communication - the other half involves listening skills. In theory, this should be the easier part, but in reality, being a good listener takes practice, too. When someone's sharing their perspectives and feelings, we may be eager to clarify our position, or to point out their misunderstandings, especially when general and social anxiety tends to never be short for NDs.

However, rushing into speaking often means cutting the speaker off, and may lead to them feeling invalidated or disrespected, and potentially a rupture in your communication and connection. Just like the seesaw analogy from Chap. 4, both parties need to have, and to give each other a chance to express their respective thoughts and feelings in healthy communication. Which is why, NDs, let's *resist* jumping in and take a deep breath together.

Of course, you're not going to be left hanging without any support on how to ensure you still communicate your perspectives without cutting the other person off. We'll discuss some practical strategies in the next sections. But for now, let's focus on the strategies that help prevent us from interrupting others when they're opening up to us about their thoughts.

Awareness is key – try to notice the sense of urgency in your body in the split second when you're in a rush to share your perspective. For some, it may be the tightening of your throat. For others, it may be holding your breath abruptly, and you may feel it in your chest. Or you may draw in an exceptionally large breath (hence, you may feel it in your torso), in preparation to deliver a big speech.

For some NDs, our brains may work like a car with a Ferrari engine but paired with bicycle breaks, and so, this can feel somewhat tricky. That's OK – with practice, we'd find that even a split-second delay before we start speaking can help with our awareness. Learn to notice your body's unique cues when you're eager to speak, then take a slow, steady breath in, and out (or three). That can be your cue for yourself to enter your 'listening mode'.

Being a good listener with executive functioning challenges

Being a good listener can be especially challenging for NDs who struggle with executive functioning (especially with working memory and inhibition). You might remember from Chap. 1 that even though executive dysfunction is a hallmark ADHD, it's not a struggle that's exclusive to ADHD. Many autistic people also struggle, to varying degrees, with different areas of their executive functioning.

A commonly reported concern for people with executive functioning challenges in this context is the worry that the very important points they'd like to make might just slip away, if they don't say it as soon as they thought of it. Or that they might forget to circle back to address an important point made by the speaker at a later time.

If that's you, try to get into the habit of taking notes (of both the speaker's main points and your thoughts) when discussing an important matter. Jot down just a few key words to help jog your memory – remember, it just needs to make sense to you! You can carry a pen and notepad with you, or simply use the Notes app on your phone.

But first, remember to communicate with the speaker (especially if you will be typing on your phone) that you're trying out a new strategy to better focus on the conversation. An example of what you might consider saying may be, *"Hey, before you go on, I'd like you to know that I'm trying out a new listening strategy and will be jotting some notes on my phone as you speak to avoid getting distracted from trying to hold all the information in my mind."*

It'd also be good practice for NDs to make notes about the main points raised by the speaker in important conversations. This will take a significant load off your working memory because you won't have to hold all the important information in your mind. It can be especially helpful in lengthy conversations that pose a high mental load.

To avoid confusion about who made which points on your notes, you can come up with your very own system with symbols to help you differentiate them. For instance, you can draw a '+' sign for the points you want to remember making later on (crossing out the ones you've communicated along the way and drawing a big star next to the ones you want to be sure you don't forget), and a 'o' sign for the speaker's main points. *In what ways, if any, does your executive functioning affect your confidence and capacity both as a speaker and a listener?*

_____

_____

_____

_____

_____

*Have you already been using any executive functioning strategies that you found helpful for your communication? If so, what are they?*_____

_____

_____

_____

_____

Active listening

Any good listening will first involve passive listening, which is giving the other party a chance to speak their mind without interrupting. Nonetheless, passive listening alone is generally insufficient if it's a long, in-depth discussion, especially in situations where you're trying to resolve disagreements or conflicts with someone (which is arguably the most challenging type of communication). Practising active listening can be useful for improving the health of your communication and relationships.

Remember, if you're feeling extremely angry or upset about something, it's typically not the right time to initiate the kind of conversations that involve active listening. Instead, practice assertively letting the other party know that you're too emotional right now to have a healthy, productive discussion, and suggest revisiting the discussion when you've both had some time to calm down

<u>and collect your thoughts.</u> A person you're in a healthy relationship with would respect that, instead of pushing you to talk.

If you have situational mutism or struggle with verbalising your thoughts when you feel very emotional, consider making a wallet-sized communication card with a simple sentence resembling the underlined sentence from the previous paragraph. Carry it in your wallet, so you'd always have it with you to show to someone else if ever needed. You can choose to laminate your communication card if you'd like for it to be more durable.

If you carry a few communication cards for different purposes around with you, you can punch a hole of the top left corner of the cards and connect the stack of cards together using a hinged ring (you can buy them from your local stationery stores). Alternatively, make a digital version of the communication card and keep it in a specific folder on your phone. This way, you can still assert your needs even under stressful circumstances, and hopefully take a break from the situation without the pressure to verbalise.

Calmly sharing how you genuinely feel (including feelings of anger) is part of being assertive. *Behaving* in an aggressive manner when feeling angry is a different matter. Or, if it's impossible to contain the aggression in the moment, try walking away from the situation. It's usually easier to come back and repair any impact from an abrupt exit than from hurtful words uttered. Regardless of neurotype, active listening is an acquired skill that requires practice. If you're completely new to this, it may even feel relatively unnatural or awkward for a while.

The good news? Many NDs find it harder to 'not do anything' (e.g., meditating, long periods of passive listening) than it is to be actively doing something. Active listening requires you to not only hold what you hear in your short-term memory, but also to manipulate the information in a meaningful way. Which means doing this can help you exercise your working memory along the way to help keep your brain actively engaged and keep you focused). Flip to the next page to learn more about it, and for examples of ways to apply different active listening strategies (*they're not exclusively/only for conflict resolution!).

IN CONFLICT RESOLUTION

Active engagement in the listening process, and not just simply hearing the other person (i.e., *purely* 'passive listening').

Benefits

1. Helps you gain a deeper understanding of the other person's perspective (regardless of whether you agree), and
2. Creates regular check points with the other person on whether you're understanding them correctly.
Basic active listening strategies below:

1.   PARAPHRASING

Repeating what the other person said using your own words, at regular intervals

Benefits

- Prevents you from prematurely jumping to solution–giving.
- Helps speaker feel heard and more motivated to continue opening up.
- Deepens your understanding and helps maintain your focus during conversation.

Examples

- "So, what you're trying to say is..."
- "If I'm hearing you correctly..."
- "What I'm hearing is..."
- "Sounds like what you see as the main issue is..."

2.   REFLECTING

Attempt to make meaningful connections between the said and unsaid and show/check in on your emotional understanding. *(Continue on the next page...)*

(...Continuing from the previous page)

Examples

- "I'm getting the sense from how you talked about X that it makes you feel..., is that right?"
- "To me, it sounds like you were more disappointed than angry about..."
- "Tell me if I'm wrong – it seems that you struggle a lot when I..."
- "Would you agree that what seems to really trouble you is..."

3. CLARIFYING

Ask for explanations/elaborations whenever you're unclear about something said.

Examples

- "I'm not quite sure I understand when you said..., can you explain that in a different way?"
- "Can you please elaborate on what you meant when you said..."

4. SUMMARISING

Consolidate main points (i.e.,thoughts and feelings) from all that has been said before ending the conversation.

Benefits

Helps both listener and speaker:
- Make sure they're on the same page
- Identify what matters the most to them in the conversation overall.

Examples

- "All in all, I heard your 3 key concerns are..."
- "You've given me quite a bit to process. Before that, let's see if I've got all your main points..."
- "Let me try to summarise what we discussed so far."

Have you ever been on either end of a conversation that involved active listening? How would you describe your experience? If not, try practising with your safe person using topics suitable for practice (e.g., starting with more emotionally neutral conversation topics). _____

_____

_____

_____

7.

NEURODIVERGENT EMOTIONS & MENTAL HEALTH

We'll be looking at all things emotional this chapter (fun stuff, I know). Building a sound understanding of some differences in the neurodivergent emotional experience is important, since our relationships with our emotions play such a big part on our mental health. A summary of last chapter's topic on healthy communication before we start:

- What assertive communication is and isn't, as well as some reasons why late-identified NDs may struggle with it.
- Verbal and non-verbal assertive communication strategies.
- Active listening strategies to be a more effective listener.

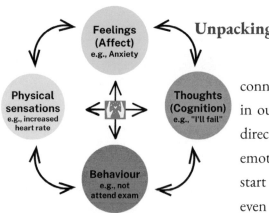

Unpacking the Emotional Experience

Notice how all the arrows connecting these 4 elements involved in our emotional experiences are bi-directional? This means that an emotional experience can literally start from any of these elements (yes, even from physical sensations). For example, it's relatively common for ADHD-ers who are trialling psychostimulant medications prescribed by their psychiatrists for the first time, to not be informed about all the common symptoms that they might experience. When the body is still adapting to the ADHD medication, many often experience increased heart rate (a physical sensation). Because they weren't expecting that, many mistake it as an anxiety symptom they associated heart palpitations with anxiety. So, they formed the impression (thoughts/cognition) that the medication caused them bad anxiety.

Because of that anxiety-provoking thought, they understandably do start feeling anxious about what they thought to be anxiety (feelings/emotions/affect). And they might stop taking the medication as a result (behaviour), and their heart rate falls back to baseline after some time. Some of them who struggle more with tolerating anxiety may not want to try the medication again to avoid that experience. However, that also means they likely have to continue enduring all the struggles that come with unmedicated ADHD, which unfortunately also leads to more stress and anxiety.

Or, at times, we might have a sudden, distressing thought, such as "I am unworthy" (thought/cognition). Immediately, we might experience a sense of anguish (emotion), which also manifests physically (e.g., aching chest, hollowness in our gut, etc). And perhaps, we react to this emotional experience by launching straight back into (over)work, instead of taking appropriate rest, in hopes that we could keep hitting our next career target and keep this horrible emotional experience at bay.

However, if we do this long enough, we might burnout and make mistakes and experience bigger setbacks at work and in life. Because we've been using this one way to try to avoid the agonising feeling associated with thoughts of unworthiness, when this happens, we're most likely going to feel an even deeper sense of anguish and unworthiness. This means that each of the four elements in the diagram above also has the potential of reinforcing each other in any and all directions. By now, you'd probably have realised that the emotions (and the corresponding physical sensations), as unpleasant as they may be, are not the issue – our behaviours that follow in our attempt to be rid of those emotions, however, can often be the issue. The more we try to 'get rid' of certain emotions, the more we end up experiencing them.

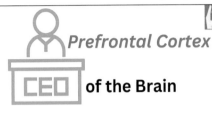

Prefrontal Cortex

CEO of the Brain

- The bit that us humans take a lot of pride in having developed.
- Role: Does everything a CEO of a company would do, including:
  - Planning and organising,
  - Decision-making,
  - Higher-level thinking and analysing,
  - Giving instructions and ensuring smooth operations.

Amygdala

'Fight-flight-freeze Centre' of the Brain

- The bit that generally cops the most hate from us humans.
- Role: To keep us alive, is all.
- But more specifically, it's a part of a system which (non-exhaustive):
  - Activates the fight-or-flight response,
  - Forms emotional memories (for strong emotions, including strongly pleasant ones).

Above: Infographic introducing the 2 main parts of the human brain involved in emotional reaction and regulation.

"All Emotions Are OK, though Not All Behaviours Are"

When I was teaching, there were often looks of disbelief when I said "all emotions are OK". But hear me out – our emotions and actions are two closely related *but distinct* entities. Each and every one of our emotions is a 'messenger' to us, much like pain is. No one likes to be in pain, but what if we lost the ability to register pain? In fact, this is a real condition called congenital insensitivity to pain with anhidrosis (CIPA). It's very rare and dangerous because it means you can't immediately tell if you touched something very hot, if you got frostbite (until you see them) or had a fracture, and must constantly check for cuts, bruises, and other possible unfelt injuries.

Think that's a bit hard to relate to? Then consider a situation that most of us would have encountered at some point: taking Panadol for gastric pains or headaches. But what if this pain is recurrent and perhaps even coming back stronger, and we just keep taking Panadol (or more Panadol) to get rid of the pain? Pain is a messenger that something needs our (or medical) attention. Getting rid of the messenger doesn't get rid of the problem.

Emotions are the same – they're trying to tell us something important about our current experience. There are, hence, no 'positive' or 'negative', 'right' or 'wrong', 'good' or 'bad' emotions per se. A healthy, functioning human being needs to be able to experience a full range of emotions. Sure, they can be varying degrees of unpleasantness or discomfort for us at different times, which affects how much we *like* an emotion. Take fear, for instance:

In a similar fashion, our sadness tells us the things that are important to us, that give us meaning in our lives. Anger tells us when our boundaries have been crossed or violated, and helps mobilise resources within our bodies to help us take action to protect and defend ourselves or our loved ones. To truly get this point across, imagine if you were told that there's a pill you could take that lets you feel happiness, and only happiness, so that you never feel all other emotions again. Even when the love of your life eventually passes away, or if someone random were to walk up to you on the street and punch you in the face, breaking your nose, you'd still be as jolly as ever.

If you just cringed at the idea, that's right. As much as we may fantasise about a happily-ever-after life, *it does not work*. Without the full range of human emotions, it'll be a life completely devoid of meaning and purpose. Now, to practice some more, let's try to decipher the potential messages within the emotions in these scenarios experienced by made-up characters:

1.   Pat feels sad that it's the last day of operation for her 6-year-old business that she built. Possible message for Pat, from her *Sadness*:

_____

_____

_____

2.   Sam is angry that his boss keeps putting off his meeting request to discuss his scheduled promotion. Possible message for Sam, from his *Anger*:

_____

_____

_____

3.   Jim feels anxious about using public transport and potentially running into unexpected service changes and being late for his appointments. Possible message for Jim, from his *Anxiety*: _____

_____

_____

_____

Hopefully this exercise helps you understand that even if it's a stretch to say that we 'love' or even 'like' all our emotions, they're an indispensable part of being human. We have a far better chance at a semi-decent relationship with our emotions, if we could practice acknowledging and respecting them, and being thankful for the 'messages' they're trying to send us. *How would you describe your relationship with your difficult emotions so far?*_____

_____

_____

_____

(Continue on the next page)

Would you say that relationship has been working for you? Why or why not?

If your relationship with your challenging emotions hasn't exactly been working for you, you're certainly not alone. See if you can write a short, personalised note for each of your main emotions below. Be honest about how you currently see them. We can struggle with something _and_ be thankful for it at the same time, with some practice. They don't have to be mutually exclusive.

To my anxiety:

I think of you as…

Thank you for…

To my sadness:

I think of you as…

Thank you for…

Having said all that, emotions don't dictate or justify any behaviours we may choose to engage in. For example, it's OK (and even necessary/healthy) to feel anger, but it's *not OK* to assault someone. The irony of treating uncomfortable emotions as 'unacceptable' or 'bad' things to be eliminated or controlled is that the attempt itself (i.e., our behaviours) often amplifies or prolong the emotional experience that we're trying so hard to curb. Check out the comic illustrating this point on the next page.

ND Differences in Emotional Awareness, Understanding, Regulation and Expression

Many NDs, especially late-identified NDs, may have been described as 'going from 0 to 100', 'over-reactive' or 'flying off the handle easily' at some point in their lives. Conversely, some others may have been accused of being 'cold', 'unemotional' or 'unempathetic', even though they really weren't, and may just have a very different expression of empathy and emotions from what others expected. These judgements are, understandably, hurtful and harmful.

(Continue reading after comic)

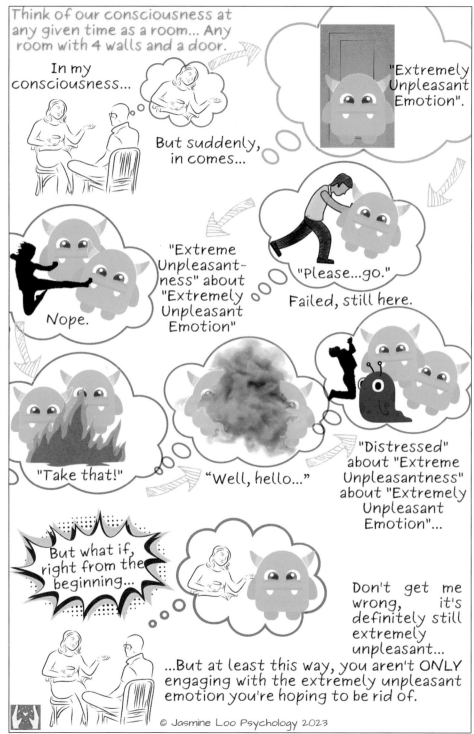

ND differences in emotional experience are, once again, a difficult thing to explain in a way that people can truly 'get' – beyond just 'knowing' cognitively, but let's have a go at this together with a fun experiment. Read the excerpt below, which describes a made-up pastry.

> *"Flower pastry can be very diverse in taste and texture. In general, flower pastries consist of a thick, soft and crumbly pastry skin enveloping a sweet, dense filling (though savoury versions are quite common). The skin is a lovely golden-brown colour, and its filling can be made of seed paste, bean paste, or other fillings using nuts like almonds or cashews (fresh/ ground). Some flower pastries may have whole seeds or nuts mixed in its filling. Their shapes are generally depictions of flowers in round/square forms."*

If I were to ask you to study the properties of flower pastries really hard – with enough time and practice, would you likely be able to pass test on flower pastries, or perhaps recite the excerpt above from memory? Most of us would probably be able to if we give it our all because of our cognitive ability to learn new information. Now, pretend you're now so familiar with information on flower pastries that you're a walking encyclopaedia of flower pastries, but have never come across a single one in real life.

Time for the reveal: Would you have recognised <u>this</u> (check out the answer on pg. 139 in the Appendix for the answer *after* you've contemplated this; no cheating!) to be a flower pastry when you see it walking past a shop front one day? Or, what if you ate it unsuspectingly once when you were very hungry, and just happened to find a flower pastry in the office pantry (shhh, we won't tell)? Would you likely have recognised what you just ate?

Never say never, but chances are, the likelihood of you **not** immediately recognising it (if at all) would be higher than the opposite. This is rather like the difference between cognitive learning and experiential knowledge of our different emotions as they arise. Except with emotional experiences, access to your prefrontal cortex (the CEO of the brain that helps you analyse what you learnt and how it can be applied to your current situation; c.f. infographic on pg. 108) may or may not be cut off at the time, depending on the intensity

114

of that emotional experience and whether consequently, your fight-flight-freeze response has been activated.

This is also one of the reasons why many NDs, especially undiagnosed NDs, may have years of therapy and become 'walking encyclopaedias' of emotions/emotional regulation, but still struggle to self-regulate when they needed it. They may not be aware of their emotional experience until it's too late – their fight-flight-freeze response has been activated and the CEO of the brain is offline. What's worse – to outsiders who think of you as having PhDs in emotions because you always seem so knowledgeable about it all, your struggles may be misunderstood or completely unknown.

Alexithymia: What Is It and How Does It Impact You?

"What do you mean?
I feel fine."
(and believe I do)

Is one of your most dreaded questions, "How does that make you feel?" Your go-to answer may be, "I don't know". You truly don't. You might know it when you are feeling angry, feeling 'good', or 'bad', but can't elaborate beyond that. Your head might start to spin when you look at the emotion wheel and see 10 times more emotion words than you've used on yourself in your lifetime, and its colours simply blur into a blinding white light. Or, you might talk and talk about your feelings with someone in your usual articulateness, but still unable to fully express how you truly felt. It's still not quite *right* no matter how much you try. How do people *know* what they're feeling *inside*, exactly?

This is what many people with alexithymia experience – an emotional blindness. Alexithymia is defined as difficulties in recognising, distinguishing and describing feelings from the bodily sensations of emotional arousal. It's a spectrum trait – you may experience all of the traits in the diagram on the next page, or only some aspects but not others, and to varying degrees.

Here comes the problem with alexithymia: How do we begin to regulate our emotions when we didn't know that we need to, often until it's too late (i.e., the CEO of the brain goes offline)? Challenges in picking up on the different

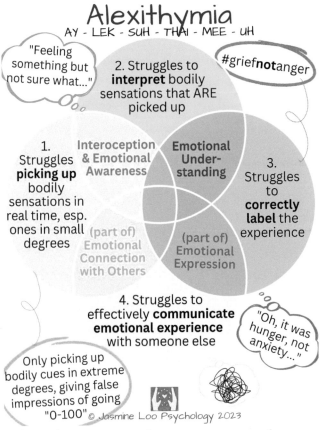

Alexithymia
AY - LEK - SUH - THAI - MEE - UH

"Feeling something but not sure what..."

2. Struggles to **interpret** bodily sensations that ARE picked up

#grief**not**anger

1. Struggles **picking up** bodily sensations in real time, esp. ones in small degrees

Interoception & Emotional Awareness

Emotional Under-standing

3. Struggles to **correctly label** the experience

(part of) Emotional Connection with Others

(part of) Emotional Expression

4. Struggles to effectively **communicate** emotional experience with someone else

"Oh, it was hunger, not anxiety..."

Only picking up bodily cues in extreme degrees, giving false impressions of going "0-100" © Jasmine Loo Psychology 2023

emotional states and intensities would mean that someone may seem like they are jumping from 0 to 100, drawing unwanted attention to themselves, creating more stress and anxiety. But in fact, they just often aren't aware of (nor do they express) 0 to, say, 70, when the CEO of their brain is still 'online'.

Alexithymia also tends to be distressing and anxiety provoking because it can mean lacking the appropriate language to express how one feels. It can mean that someone with the trait is unable to "empty their chest", or to move onto problem solving mode (to be fair, how could anyone solve a problem they don't really understand?), or to get the help they need because they have trouble articulating what they are struggling with.

Experiencing alexithymia doesn't necessarily mean that a person can't answer questions such as 'what would person A most likely be feeling in scenario X?' Most people can learn to answer questions like these. But do they know how sadness or disappointment feels in their bodies as they are experiencing those emotions? This is the reason for the flower pastry experiment in the previous section – to demonstrate the differences between one's cognitive knowledge and experiential knowledge of the very same thing.

Interestingly, researchers studying brain metabolic activity using functional magnetic resonance imaging (fMRI) found that by simply being able to correctly label the emotions that we are feeling, negative emotional reactions can be significantly reduced when exposed to negative emotion triggers. Considering all this, it's perhaps not surprising at all that higher levels of alexithymia are linked to higher self-reported anxiety, depression, atypical sensory modulation, and informant-reported emotional difficulties.

What's more, emotional labeling was shown to produce a pattern of neural responses similar to those seen when a person engages in intentional emotional regulatory strategies taught in Cognitive Behavioural Therapy (CBT), even *without* having used any CBT strategies. This doesn't mean that we'd stop experiencing a certain emotion simply from effective affect labeling, but that we're less likely to *involuntarily react* to our emotions.

Did you know? Alexithymia affects an estimated 40-65% of autistic individuals, and affects approximately 22% of adult ADHDers, compared to approximately 10% of neurotypicals (even though research in alexithymia and ADHD is very sparse; to date, there are only 2 research studies conducted by the same group of German researchers).

So far, studies done on ADHD and alexithymia found the underlying third factor connecting these two seems to be the tendency to reject one's emotions (fancy scientific term for this is 'experiential avoidance'). This is supported by other research discovering that people with higher levels of alexithymia tend to show stronger non-acceptance of (primarily unpleasant) emotions and poorer emotional regulation. Remember the comic strip featuring the "extremely unpleasant emotion" on pg. 113?

Alexithymic ADHDers may be especially disadvantaged here, since avoidance is a common struggle for many ADHDers. This may be partly why many ADHDers find therapy approaches like Acceptance and Commitment Therapy (ACT) more helpful because of its focus on improving tolerance (rather than avoidance) of unpleasant emotions, just like the comic from earlier.

Rate the following on a scale of 1-10 (1 = 'Not at all' to 10 = 'Extremely so').

Generally, how hard is it for you to...

♦ *Make sense of your feelings <u>in the moment</u> that you're experiencing them?*

♦ *Differentiate between your thoughts, emotions and body sensations?*

♦ *Put your feelings into words and communicate them accurately with others?*

♦ *Be aware of the cues that your body sends you <u>in a timely manner</u> and use them to tell you what you may be feeling?*

How frequently do you...

♦ *Believe that your behaviours are dictated by emotions, or that they're one and the same?*

♦ *Spend long periods of time trying to 'get rid' of an unpleasant emotion?*

♦ *Find others misunderstanding how you feel about something or the actual degree that you feel an emotion, but struggle to make clarifications?*

♦ *In retrospect, realise that you completely misinterpreted your own feelings or emotions?*

If you've just learnt something new about yourself, note your reflections below:

_____

_____

_____

If your self-ratings above are high (suggesting some struggles with emotional awareness and understanding), consider incorporating emotional literacy as a therapy goal in your work with your therapist. Or if you aren't currently seeing a professional, consider seeking support in this area from a psychologist with a solid understanding of late-identified neurodivergence.

Emotional literacy is all about the continuous learning of the finer, distinct elements involved in our emotional experiences. It's just like how as children, we may learn about the colour 'purple'. But as we grow, especially if we become more knowledgeable about colours, we may learn about the different shades of purple, (e.g., lilac, violet, fuchsia) and what different effects could be achieved by mixing a certain shade of purple with another colour.

Thoughts

Can be in the form of:
- Memory
- Pictures or images
- Words (ideas or opinions, self-talk, etc)
- Moving pictures (like a video recording)

Whether we realise it or not, our brains are 'thought generators' - spewing thoughts throughout the day.

Occur in the parts of our brain that evolved later (neocortex in the frontal lobe region).

Thoughts are a 'time-traveller' - we can have thoughts about any time in the past or the future, not just the immediate present.

Emotions

Can be in the form of:
- Feelings or sentiments   - Mood

Involve physiological or bodily changes (arousal levels and/or physical sensations).

The fight-or-flight reactions occur in the more primitive parts of our brain (limbic system), but emotional regulation similarly happens in the neocortex.

Under most circumstances, our bodies and the body cues we pick up are rooted in the immediate present.

A large part of emotional regulation relies on our capacities in (1) picking up associated bodily cues as they're happening, and (2) in making sense of them.

Above: Infographic showing differences between our thoughts & emotions.

Empathy in the context of neurodivergence & alexithymia

Empathy, which is essential for social functioning, is defined as the capacity of understanding and sharing others' emotions. It can be categorised into cognitive (discussed in Chap. 1) and *emotional empathy*, which is how we share and feel emotions that others are experiencing, discussed below.

Many NDs of different presentations would have been accused of 'lacking empathy' to varying frequencies in their lives, perhaps even by people they share close relationships with. While there's consistent scientific finding that perspective-taking may not come naturally for many autistic people, the hurt from a generalised label of "unempathetic" tends to be capable of reaching to the very core of a person's existence. But what does science say about this? (Spoiler: science debunked this myth).

In 2022, a group of researchers examined the 2 sub-components of emotional empathy - empathic concern (EC) and personal distress (PD) – along with alexithymia severity in autistic people. They found that in the ASD group, *higher* levels of comorbid *alexithymia* were linked to (1) lower empathic concerns (i.e., self-reports of fewer physical sensations during emotional experience; I mean, of course, that's the very definition of alexithymia), *but, hang on, also* (2) higher levels of personal distress to others' emotions.

What this demonstrates is that while autistics with alexithymia may experience and express emotional empathy *differently*, it should *not* be characterised as an absence of capacity for emotional empathy. We need more community education to bust harmful myths, such as "being autistic means no empathy"; these scientific findings encapsulate this perfectly. In fact, research suggests that there are more NDs who are hyper-empathetic, experiencing so much empathy for others that they struggle to separate others' emotions or pain and their own, until their empathy feels paralysing to them.

All in all, does this mean that all NDs are empathetic? No! But generalisations, especially unfounded ones, can cause significant harm to the people involved. There are NDs who are more empathetic and less empathetic in their own ways, and there are NTs who are more empathetic and less empathetic. Ultimately, we're all humans, who together form *neurodiversity*.

Research on alexithymia and ADHD, as we touched on previously, remains sparse, and research on ADHD and empathy and theory of mind is little to nil currently, as found in a systematic review published last year in 2022. If you're familiar with the field of research and academia, you might know of the sad reality that emphases of research topics have less to do with the importance of the topic, or the amount of people affected by it, and more with where the research funding goes.

Because of the lack of research, it's still tricky to draw confident conclusions one way or another, but some scientists hypothesised that the executive dysfunction of some ADHDers may affect their capacity to accurately decipher others' emotions. Nonetheless, I wouldn't be surprised at all if similar findings to that of the 2022 autism study above would be discovered, if and when there are a decent number of quality research studies done on the subject matter. *What's your overall experience with empathy (e.g., no difficulties/ struggling with having too much of it/ being seen as not having enough of it, etc)?*

_____

_____

_____

_____

*Do you think alexithymia creates any difficulties for you in showing others empathy in a way they understand?*_____

_____

_____

_____

_____

*If you struggle with empathy in any ways at all, is there anyone who can help you change your narrative with your empathy? e.g., marriage counsellor to help you better understand empathetic expressions that your spouse is receptive to, or a therapist to help you develop healthy boundaries from others' emotions, etc.*_____

_____

_____

_____

Exercises to Build Emotional Awareness and Understanding

If you struggle with emotion wheels, this way of conceptualising emotions in the diagram on the next page might be more helpful. Think of your emotions as being in 4 quadrants, based on: x-axis = degree of pleasantness, and y-axis = energy level (low to high). Can you come up with more emotion words that you can relate to in each quadrant on the diagram on the next page? Write them in the relevant quadrants. You can refer to the 'cheat sheet' on pg. 51, which contains lists of emotion words, if you'd like some ideas.

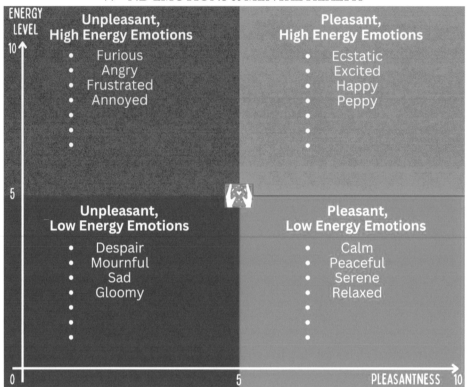

Next, in each of the colour gradients on the following pages, try thinking about something (can be an event, a memory, an activity, etc) that makes you feel different degrees of the corresponding emotion, and write them down. There's no one right way to tackle the activity, but if you find it slightly challenging, try to start with the superlatives (i.e., Level 7 / darkest colour gradient: things that make you the happiest/saddest, etc), then think of something that makes you feel the mildest level of those emotions (i.e., Level 1 / lightest colour gradient).

Then, move onto thinking about something that made you feel moderate levels of the emotion (Level 4) before filling out the rest (Levels 2 & 3, 5 & 6). If you'd like to, you can also select descriptive words from the lists on both sides of the colour gradients that you think best describe what how you feel based on the event that you filled out on each level. For both this activity and the Body Scanner activity on pg. 125, remember to scan the QR code (instructions in Introduction) to download the full-sized sheets for free, so you can do a separate Body Scanner sheet for each emotion. These are just provided for your reference.

DEGREES OF My Joy

(And lists of descriptors to help you express yourself)

Pleased	
Cheery	
Peppy	Jolly
Excited	Upbeat
Satisfied	Confident
Ecstatic	Joyful
Proud	Cheerful
Euphoric	Exhilarated
Positive	On cloud 9
Glad	Delighted
Gleeful	Chirpy
On top of the world	Lively
	Chipper
	In high spirits

DEGREES OF My Sadness

(And lists of descriptors to help you express yourself)

Hurt	
Lost	
In anguish	Despair
Dispirited	Empty
Sorrowful	Dejected
Depressed	Tearful
Unmotivated	Lonely
Discouraged	Unhappy
Heartbroken	Deflated
Vulnerable	Defeated
Miserable	Hopeless
Disillusioned	Weary
Devastated	Mournful
Dissatisfied	
Uninspired	
Pessimistic	

123

DEGREES OF My Anger

(And lists of descriptors to help you express yourself)

Irritated	Cranky
Annoyed	Insulted
Offended	Grumpy
Frustrated	Worked up
Enraged	Crossed
Irritable	Boiling
Sulky	Resentful
Fuming	Indignant
Aggravated	Raging
Infuriated	Furious
Exasperated	Outraged
Irritable	Aggrieved
P****d off*	

*Not for everyone, but for those who are interested, refer to the bibliography page for research on the benefits of swearing

DEGREES OF My Anxiety

(And lists of descriptors to help you express yourself)

Shaky	Apprehensive
Worried	Uneasy
Nervous	Overwhelmed
Anxious	Exhilarated
Restless	Frightened
Shocked	Terrified
Insecure	Alarmed
Ruminative	Horrified
Restless	Preoccupied
Wary	Uncertain
Scared	
Stressed	
Fearful	

(NAME OF EMOTION) Body Scanner

Imagine going into a body scanner when you're experiencing the emotion above, much like the airport security scanners. Except, instead of picking up metals, this scanner picks up the changes within your body. This includes all your body sensations (e.g., hot face, faster heart rate) and body-based behaviours from head to toe (e.g., holding breath, clenching fists, etc) that occurs when you're experiencing the emotion. Label them below in 2 different colours: one for when you're feeling the emotion mildly, the other for when you're feeling the same emotion strongly.

EXAMPLE Sadness Body Scanner

REMEMBER, EVERYONE EXPERIENCES SADNESS DIFFERENTLY!

Imagine going into a body scanner when you're experiencing the emotion above, much like the airport security scanners. Except, instead of picking up metals, this scanner picks up the changes within your body. This includes all your body sensations (e.g., hot face, faster heart rate) and body-based behaviours from head to toe (e.g., holding breath, clenching fists, etc) that occurs when you're experiencing the emotion. Label them below in 2 different colours: one for when you're feeling the emotion mildly, the other for when you're feeling the same emotion strongly.

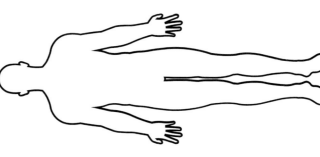

Mildly

Teary/ crying
Often have downcast eyes
Taking deep breaths more frequently
Shoulders slumped
Heart 'sinks'
Low energy, more tired
Sleeps a bit more/ less than usual
Footsteps feel heavier than usual

Strongly

Frequent crying & sobbing / unable to cry
Breathlessness
Tension in neck & shoulders
Emptiness/ pain in chest
Exhaustion (general & social)
Hollowness in stomach
Whole body feels heavy
Lack of desire to move body

8.

LIVING YOUR VALUED NEURODIVERGENT LIFE

In Chap. 3 (or the first chapter in Section II), we reflected on your past with ND lenses. In our final chapter, we'll be looking at the way forward. But first, let's quickly recap what the last chapter was all about:

- Emotional literacy 101, and the foundation of what happens in our brain during emotional experiences.
- Alexithymia and its link to neurodivergence: What it means for ND emotional awareness and understanding, and mental health.
- Alternative perspectives to help us change our relationships with our difficult emotions.

What Makes It Worth Your While, NDs?

Some of you might recall the famous words of my mentor from Chap. 6, on life being a series of trade-offs. And in Chap. 7, we established that as much as we may wish we could feel happy *all the time*, not only is that wishful thinking, but even if it's plausible, life would be completely devoid of any meaning. Real life is a complete package, filled with the good, the bad, and a whole lot of mundane interspersed in between. No matter how awesome, wise, successful a person we are, or may become, it doesn't change that fact. The world can be full of injustice, but this bit is at least somewhat fair, since no one can be exempt from it.

In Chap. 7, we discussed why it's the *process* in which we attempt to avoid the unavoidable parts of life that often creates the psychological pain that just keeps snowballing, instead of helping us feel any happier. So, if unpleasantness, discomfort, distress and even pain are inevitable in life, my big question for all of you is... *"What makes it worth your while?"*

Not fully getting my question? That's OK. Try to picture this: If I were to tell you that there's a relatively hefty fee that you have no choice but to pay every month for the rest of your lives, what would likely be your first, immediate response? If you thought, "What for??", that's *exactly* right! As humans, we aren't usually happy to simply go along with things, especially unpleasant things we don't like, without a reason that makes sense to us.

So, if I were to tell you, "No particular reason, you just HAVE to", you wouldn't be very happy with me, would you? Bear in mind that this is still real life, so money doesn't just fall into your hands – and work can be a pain. In exchange for your time and effort, you're now paying for... nothing?? Fair enough that you're not happy about it. What if instead I said, "for your income-protection insurance?" You may not necessarily buy into the idea of insurance, and definitely still not ecstatic about the cost, but if the cost is inevitable, having a decent reason beats not having any, right?

You might think that if there's no way to wiggle out of this, at least the price that you pay, both financially and psychologically, would be in exchange for your financial security in the event that you could no longer work. In this analogy, the 'unavoidable hefty price' is parallel to the parts of life that absolutely suck but are inevitable (e.g., unpleasant / uncomfortable / distressing / painful feelings and thoughts). When the unpleasantness is in exchange for something we perceive as of value to us, it can make a huge difference to our perspectives towards life.

Now, what if instead of being told the above reason, I was to tell you that it's for making some random stranger's dream come true to be able to travel the world? Would you have felt the same way about paying that price as you did? Most probably not. This is also why it's important for us to determine our very own core values in life, in lieu of just blindly following someone else's values. No one else can live this life (and endure the worst and savour the best it has to offer) but ourselves. So, what the question above is really asking is, what are the things in life that **you decide** are worth you going through the parts that suck in life, even if you still don't like them and would rather avoid them all if you could?

Most, if not all, late-identified NDs would be no strangers to hardship in life – from simply trying to make it through another day in a world that's not designed for us to trying to build self-acceptance and a sense of belonging. Many of us may have been working hard for a long time, perhaps even most of our lives, to exist in ways, moving in directions that *others* value. It's time to consider our own life values. Staying in survival mode by being what the world may want us to be might offer some short-term positives, but it's not sustainable, and definitely won't make the unpleasant parts of life any less so.

Values Are Not the Same as Goals

If you just panicked and thought, "Arghhhh nooooo, not more goal-setting, inspirational, motivational, clichéd BS", *relax*, values and goals are not synonymous. You *won't* be asked to imagine and write about where you'd like to be in life in 5 years' time. Let's face it, even knowing what to have for dinner tonight can be a tough mountain for us to climb, pfft, forget about 5 years. It's not to say there's completely zero value in setting goals, but it's not what we're interested in, and will be focusing on here.

Goals represent <u>desired outcomes</u> that you can check off as they're being accomplished, or like the fate of most goals and New Year's resolutions, be buried under piles of other forgotten goals. Depending on the person, goals may or may not have anything to do with what the person would like to do, or even *can* do. For example, "marrying into a rich family" can technically be a goal, but most of the time, the person setting such a goal meant it more in the sense of hoping that this is something that could *simply happen to them.*

I mean, sure, who wouldn't wish to be lucky in life? But if that's what we're banking on to 'feel good' about life, we're most likely going to feel out of control and miserable much of the time. Because, chance or luck, circumstances and outcomes of different situations are beyond our circle of influence (which we'll discuss in the next section) the majority of the time.

Goals are like school or university semesters, there's always a time that they naturally end, regardless of whether you pass or flunk and have to repeat, or drop out. For NDs, goals can be dopamine-depleting or dopamine-mining, or both, at different times. But if you think about it, our goals don't always make sense when they're all lined up, since they're usually driven by what we want or wish for at any given time. For instance, if we were to line up all your past year's New Year resolutions, they might look something like this:

2018 – Land my dream job!
2019 – Work out and eat healthy
2020 – Get a raise or promotion at work (ideally both)
2021 – Travel the world :'(

We might still somewhat see the 'you' in the list, but you may notice what's missing is a *direction*. It doesn't really give us information about what you truly *care* about, what's *meaningful* and *important* for you in life. Your *values*.

Values – What They Are and Aren't

Values do not offer any check boxes that we can tick off, or a destination to arrive to, as goals would offer. Instead, values offer us a *direction,* much like Polaris, the North Star, that guides us to engage in behaviours that are in line with our values. If we think of directions, there really is no end point per se. We can technically keep going west (or whatever other directions) indefinitely.

The steps we take either bring us closer towards, or further away from our intended direction. When we think about it this way, there's no such thing as "failing" when it comes to values. Most of us would have lost our way before (especially those of us who tend to get lost even using the GPS), but we can usually get on track again eventually, once we're aware that we've gone astray.

Values are in the way we live, not what we accomplish. It's in what we choose to dedicate our efforts to, not the outcomes of said efforts. It's rooted in what's *within* our 'circle of influence' (shown on the right), not beyond. Let's say one of our core values is honesty. And how we choose to live it is by treating others, especially those

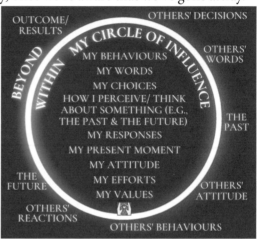

from our key relationships with openness and authenticity. This doesn't mean, however, that we can then expect others to also treat us the same way. This is because other people's actions, decisions and attitudes are always going to be outside of our circle of influence, which is not what values are about.

What our values might translate to, in real life, can look different for different people (and this is where value-directed actions come in! – more on this in the next section). For one person, it may be taking initiative to have challenging conversations with people they have a close relationship with, even if that's anxiety provoking. For another person, it may be resisting the default urge to people-please by immediately agreeing with something that someone else said, when they actually disagree.

Now that you understand what values are and aren't about, using the diagram on pg. 132, write your core values in life (the main general category). Try to limit it to no more than 3 core values because when everything's important, it means nothing's important. If you *really* struggle with choosing 3, try using the elimination method. Pretend you're on a ship and there's a leak (it's a leak you can't fix, don't go there), and you have to start chucking stuff off

Values

Kindness

Connection   Contribution   Adventure

Justice

Freedom

Love   Spirituality

Curiosity

Acceptance

Sensuality   Generosity   Assertiveness

Fun/
Humour   Dedication   Skillfulness

Pleasure

Self-
awareness

Respect

Self-care   Sexuality   Independence

to reduce the weight of the ship. Start chucking the values you picked, one by one, until you're left with 3. You can use the examples from the diagram on the left for ideas. If you have some core values that are unique to particular relationships or parts of your identity (e.g., values reflecting the friend/ parent/ learner/ partner/ spouse, or even the ND that you'd like to be), write them on the bottom part of the diagram. They can also be values specific to certain main life domains (e.g., "Career", "Health", etc.). You can ignore the bottom part of the diagram if your core life values apply to all areas of your life.

*Before this, did you already have a clear idea of your core life values?*_____

_____

_____

*Before this, have you been focusing more on elements within or beyond your circle of influence? How did that impact you?*_____

_____

_____

_____

_____

*Did you find this exercise relatively easy or difficult? Why so, do you think?*_____

_____

_____

_____

_____

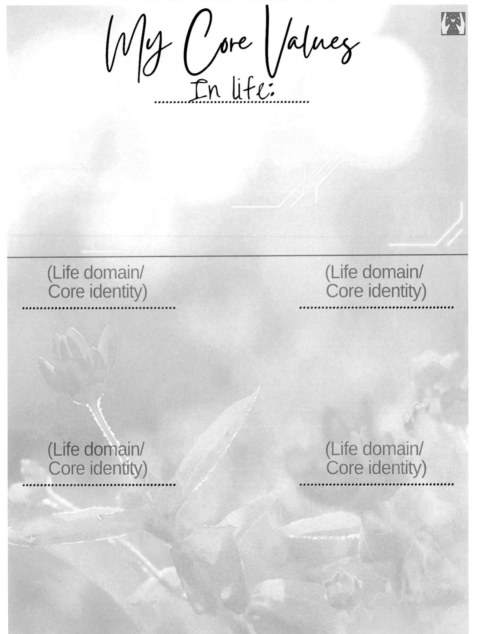

My Core Values
In life:

(Life domain/
Core identity)

(Life domain/
Core identity)

(Life domain/
Core identity)

(Life domain/
Core identity)

For those of us who may value continuously striving to be a "better person", identifying a limited number of core life values can be a huge struggle. It's a wonderful trait to always want to be better, but "being a better person" is too broad in its range to allow us to truly define what that looks like. Every person has a finite amount of time on earth, a finite amount of energy and personal resources. Time spent on one thing is time taken away from something else. Energy and effort invested in one thing is energy and effort we no longer have for something else.

Identifying our core values doesn't mean not having a single care about the other values. It just means we are focusing our finite pool of resources and time primarily on the most important things for us to create a life that we find meaningful and purposeful, even when it doesn't get any easier. At times, 2 of our core values may be in conflict with each other (e.g., caring for self vs another), and in that case, we can reflect and make a mindful decision.

Doable, Value-Directed Actions for *ND*s

It'd be wise to set targets for actions that are not only value-directed, but also doable from where we're currently standing. When our actions are not value-directed, they tend to be all over the place, like the example of New Year's resolutions we looked at previously. Even when we do 'go places', the places we go may not add up to a coherent direction, creating meaning in our lives.

When our targets for actions to be taken aren't perceived as realistic and achievable, we may struggle to even begin to fathom approaching them. Let's say someone who hasn't exercised for 9 years is being asked to climb Mount Everest tomorrow. They'd most probably think, "Not a chance". What if they allow themselves a substantial amount of time, and start building up their fitness from the very modest starting point of taking regular walks around their neighbourhood? In time, they might still think, "No way", but perhaps that idea wouldn't seem as unthinkable as it was before.

We all need to start somewhere; setting realistic targets is the very first step we take to match our efforts to our values. If we have strayed quite far away from our values in the past, starting with a small, achievable step will give us better chances, compared to a big, intimidating target. It wouldn't be surprising if some of you would think, "But I'm an all-or-nothing person;

either I don't do something, or I need to go all out. Moderation is challenging for NDs, indeed. Try contemplating these facts:

- Living without knowing its purpose and meaning for us is difficult
- Living against our values (that we've determined) is difficult
- Living only according to other people's values is difficult
- Living according to our values while sitting with our discomfort/distress of not immediately becoming the very embodiment of that value is difficult

All of these options are difficult – we've established that. The question is, which 'difficult' would you choose? If this is tough for you to answer, consider using the cost-benefit breakdown template from Chap. 6 to help you.

Do it afraid

Often in life, we're so busy trying to 'get rid of' our unpleasant emotions and thoughts that we may lose sight of our values. Using the same analogy from the last section, it'd be equivalent to spending every waking moment (and perhaps even in our dreamland) arguing why we shouldn't have to pay 'the price', trying to find ways to help us get out of paying it, and still simultaneously paying it the entire time. Fighting against something outside of our control becomes the sole focus of our lives instead.

Each moment that we're engaging in attempted avoidance of the unpleasant and painful is another moment that we're disengaging from the life that we actually want to be living. Our ND brains may want to convince us that we could multitask and do both of those things, but we really can't (even research tells us trying to multitask is a bad idea). Think of the number of times we have missed a moment 'that could have been' (whatever it may be) because we were too busy trying to stop feeling anxious, or feeling down, or feeling any other particular way? To stop thinking about something?

Don't get me wrong – there'll definitely be times when we're able to simply 'will a thought (or an emotion) away' and get back on with life. When that's the case, fantastic! Let's do that. At the same time, this definitely won't work every single time, under all different circumstances. So, *do what works*. Generally, we tend to automatically assume the following as our only options:

1. Only being able to do something when it feels 'good'/ 'right'
2. Not being able to do something when we *don't* feel good about it (i.e., anxiety/ distress that we can't shake off about doing the thing).

But what if there's a 3rd option? What if, instead, we were to radically accept the parts of the human experience that we cannot change or avoid, acknowledge that it absolutely sucks, and redirect our attention and effort to the stuff we decide is important? To do something afraid. To do something we find meaningful, even when still grieving or hurting. You get the idea.

Doing something that helps carve out the rich, meaningful life we want to live doesn't have to be dependent on the absence of thoughts and emotions we struggle with. It doesn't mean we can't rest or take time to heal from our pain (these are healthy things we DO want to do), but rather, that we don't have to *wait* until we no longer struggle to start living meaningfully. Because then, we'll never be able to start since life will always contain some element of struggle. It doesn't even have to be limited by circumstances. Say, one of our values is giving back to society. Pretend we used to generate a handsome income, and had always made substantial yearly donations to local charities.

But let's say, we then went broke for whatever reason. When our own family's survival is in question, it's understandable that we wouldn't have the capacity to donate money to others. But if we get really creative about it, there are many other ways we could possibly live according to our value to give back. Perhaps we could volunteer an hour a day at our child's school regulating traffic at pick up time? Or we might decide we have the capacity to help run the social media fundraising campaign for a charity we supported?

Then again, if we were to be completely honest, it's often easier said than done. At this point, many of us would likely be hit by a pang of anxiety or perhaps even unworthiness, "Ah... but that'll raise the conversation about why I'm no longer making donations and everyone will know I went broke. It'd be easier to just quietly fade away from the charity scene to avoid becoming embarrassed...". At this point, it'd be as if we're standing at crossroads like the cartoon below:

While none of us have any control over how the world works (or even over when our unpleasant thoughts and emotions come and go), in order for you to consider this a meaningful life that's worth all the crap it comes with, in your day-to-day, what kinds of behaviours would you be engaging in? What kinds of actions would you be taking? *How* will you be doing them?

As practice, pick one of your core values that you've identified and written on the diagram from the previous section, and reflect on a realistic way for you to be living that value this week. On the diagram below, write a short description of a value-driven behaviour (can be internal, e.g., practising making space for a difficult emotion instead of avoiding, or external behaviours) that you perceive as doable given your current circumstances.

One realistic way for me to live according to my core value of
.... this week is:

HOW DOABLE IS THIS FOR ME?

1	2	3	4	5
NOT AT ALL				YES, ABSOLUTELY!

EXAMPLE

One realistic way for me to live according to my core value of
.......Connection........... this week is:

By sending a text message to a good friend I haven't been in touch with for some time. / By attending a community painting class ⟍

Showing you 2 examples, but only write one on yours!

HOW DOABLE IS THIS FOR ME?

1	2	3	4	5
NOT AT ALL				YES, ABSOLUTELY!

If you end up giving something a doability rating of less than 4, go back to the drawing board and come up with something more bite-sized. For instance, if you wrote "sending a text message to a good friend I haven't contacted for a while", then realised your doability rating for this is only about 3, you might adapt it to something like "hitting like on one of their social media posts" to start. You can always work your way up to your original target.

This exercise is a tool to help you practice your values with mindful intention; once you're used to it, it'll come to you naturally. Remember, *every action we take counts*. If you enjoy what we've been doing with values and relationships with our emotions, consider working with a mental health practitioner experienced in delivering Acceptance and Commitment Therapy (ACT). This is just a sneak peak of the kind of work involved in ACT.

If Exploring Values Is One Step Too Far Right Now...

In Chap. 5, we touched on how many NDs may have invested much of their lives in learning how to mask as a survival mechanism in a NT world. This may leave little opportunities (esp. before learning about neurodivergence) for self-discovery, which is essential for forming a solid self-identity. When we're still in the beginning stages of learning and sculpting who we are as a person, trying to figure out our core values may seem one step too far. ***If that's you... Fear not!!!*** Remember, if the target doesn't seem doable, we adjust it! No justification necessary.

Here's an activity you can try out in your own time to help you learn more about yourself. Ideally, you'll be trying this out on your own, so there wouldn't be any perceived pressure, or distractions from another person to focus on anything else but your own perspective. If you'd really like for a support person to be with you, they can go along for emotional support, so long as they avoid interacting with you during the activity. To start, set aside a block of time (10 to 20 minutes) to take a walk outside in an area familiar to you (e.g., your local park, around the block, etc). It doesn't matter when and where, so long as it's safe for you to do so. If you'd like to, or if it helps with your focus, you can set a timer on your phone and put it on silent mode.

I'd like you to pay attention to your surroundings as you walk (literally doesn't matter which direction or turns you take – whatever you feel like at the time!), and when something catches your eye, something that holds your gaze for more than a few moments (seriously, they don't have to meet any criteria, just anything that holds your attention), snap a picture of it with the camera on your phone. Look up, look down, look everywhere around you with gentle curiosity and pay close attention to everything you come across, as if it was the first time you see it. Chances are, you'd find details you never noticed, even when you've literally walked around the area a thousand times.

When you get home, look through all the photos taken on your walk. Lay them all out in front of you if possible, and look at the lenses from which you viewed the world just then. What do these photos tell you? When there's no one telling you where to look, where and what did your gaze linger on? You know how some marine biologists would put a GoPro on a sea turtle or a seabird to see their literal point of view? Kind of like that, except you're that curious study subject. If you find this exercise interesting, try doing it some more in your day-to-day.

As you become more used to practicing mindfulness (i.e., focusing attention on your experience in the present moment), there's no need to set aside time for this. You could be snapping a photo on your commute to work, or during your evening jog. You might find, when you string all these snapshots together, a story about the person who experienced these moments may just start to emerge. This is a totally open-ended exercise (Eeee, frustrating, I know), and your guess is as good as mine on what you might find, but *that's the whole point*. I do not tell you what's worthy of your attention or what meaning to make of your experiences. *No one does, but you.*

We'll end the final topic of this book on that note.

Bibliography

For a full bibliography list for references used throughout this book, please scan the QR code below.

Appendix

Revealing the answer to the experiment on pg. 112 in Chap 7. I confess that it wasn't actually a made-up pastry, but rather a made-up name to a real pastry. If you're an Asian who's very familiar with it, you may have thought that the description sounded a bit like mooncakes. But that's really only because you're already very familiar with the experience itself.

If you're new to mooncakes and are curious about it, consider buying one if you ever come across them (they're only available at certain times of the year). Feel it, smell it, taste it, and see how close it is to your imagination when you learnt about the facts around it. That'll complete our experiential experiment.

ACKNOWLEDGMENTS

I would like to express my appreciation and acknowledge everyone who has contributed to the development of this self-help guide book, and the group therapy program that this book is birthed from:

The original Divergent Adults' Group Therapy Program participants, for providing your invaluable feedback on parts of the program materials that could benefit from further elaboration, or clarification.

Dr Shane Costello and Emmalee Stefanatos, for proof-reading and reviewing the original manuscript, and copyediting the final manuscript.

Judy Singer, autistic Australian sociologist who originally coined the term "neurodiversity" in late 1990s, and multiply neurodivergent activist, Kassiane Asasumasu, who went on to coin the terms "neurodivergent" and "neurotypical", all of which are used throughout this book.

And finally, my student, Andrea Ong, for your helpful feedback on the original group program, and for co-facilitating the group therapy program with me.

Made in the USA
Columbia, SC
22 December 2024

50480601R00084